*I am not ashamed of the gospel of Christ, for it is the power of God to salvation for everyone who believes.*
– Romans 1:16

# MOODY'S
# ADDRESSES

UPDATED EDITION

# Register This New Book

## Benefits of Registering*

- ✓ FREE **replacements** of lost or damaged books

- ✓ FREE **audiobook** – *Pilgrim's Progress,* audiobook edition

- ✓ FREE information about new titles and other **freebies**

www.anekopress.com/new-book-registration

*See our website for requirements and limitations.

MOODY'S

# ADDRESSES

## 12 SERMONS THAT WILL CHANGE YOUR LIFE

### DWIGHT L. MOODY

We enjoy hearing from our readers. Please contact us at www.anekopress.com/questions-comments with any questions, comments, or suggestions.

*Moody's Addresses*

© 2024 by Aneko Press

All rights reserved. First edition 1876.

Revisions copyright 2024.

*Cover Designer: J. Martin*

*Editor: C. Miskimen*

Aneko Press

www.anekopress.com

Aneko Press, Life Sentence Publishing, and our logos are trademarks of

Life Sentence Publishing, Inc.
203 E. Birch Street
P.O. Box 652
Abbotsford, WI 54405

**RELIGION / Faith**

Paperback ISBN: 979-8-88936-472-6

eBook ISBN: 979-8-88936-473-3

10  9  8  7  6  5  4  3  2

Available where books are sold

# CONTENTS

# PREFACE

Because many friends have asked me to do so, I have consented to the publication of the following addresses.

I deeply feel how partially and insufficiently the glorious gospel of the blessed God is represented in them, but I lay them at the Master's feet, praying and asking all my Christian friends to pray that they may be the means in their printed form of winning more souls to Christ than they have been when spoken.

# "WHERE ARE YOU?"

*Then the LORD God called to Adam*
*and said to him, "Where are you?"*
– Genesis 3:9

The very first thing that happened after the news of the fall of man reached heaven was that God came straight down to seek out the lost one. As He walked through the garden in the cool of the day, He might have been heard calling, "Adam! Adam! *Where are you?*" It was the voice of grace, of mercy, and of love. Adam ought to have taken the seeker's place, for he was the transgressor. He had fallen, and he ought to have gone up and down Eden crying, "My God! My God! Where are You?" But God left heaven to seek through the dark world for the rebel who had fallen – not to hurl him from the face of the earth but to plan for him a way of escape from the misery of his sin. And He found him – where? Hiding from his Creator among the bushes of the garden.

The moment a man, even a professed child of God, is out of communion with God, he wants to hide from Him. When God left Adam in the garden, he was in communion with his

Creator, and God talked with him; but now that he had fallen, he had no desire to see his Creator. He had lost communion with his God. He could not bear to see Him nor even to think of Him, and he ran to hide from God. But to his hiding place his Maker followed him: "Where are you, Adam? Where are you?"

Thousands of years have passed, and this text has come down through the ages. I doubt whether there has been any one of Adam's sons who has not heard it at some period or other of his life – stealing over him sometimes in the midnight hour: "Where am I? Who am I? Where am I going? And what will be the end of this?" I think it is good for a man to pause and ask himself the question of my text. You ask it, little boy; and you, little girl; and you, old man with hair turning gray, eyes growing dim, and strength fading – you who will soon be in another world. I do not ask you where you are in the eyes of your neighbors. I do not ask you where you are in the eyes of your friends. I do not ask you where you are in the eyes of the community in which you live. It matters little where we are in the eyes of one another. It is of very little account what men think of us, but it is of vast importance what *God* thinks of us – it is of vast importance to know where men are in the eyes of God. That is the question now.

Am I in communion with my Creator or out of communion? If I am out of communion, there is no peace, no joy, no happiness. No man on the face of the earth who was out of communion with his Creator ever knew what peace, joy, happiness, and true comfort were. He is a stranger to them. But when we are in communion with God, there is light all around our path. So ask yourselves this question. Do not think I am preaching to your neighbors, but remember I am trying to speak to you, to every one of you as if you were alone. It was the first question put to man after his fall, and it was a very small audience that God had – Adam and his wife. But God was the preacher, and although they tried to hide, the words came home to them. Let them come home to you now. You may think that your life is hidden, that God does not know anything about you. But He knows our lives much better than we do, and His eye has been fixed on us from our earliest childhood until now.

I will divide my audience into three groups – the professed Christians, the backsliders, and the ungodly. First, I would like to ask each one who professes Christ this question or rather, let God ask it – Where are you? What is your position in the church and among your acquaintances? Do your friends know you to be out and out on the Lord's side? You may have been a professing Christian for twenty years, perhaps thirty or forty years, but where are you tonight? Are you making progress toward heaven? Can you

*Are you making progress toward heaven?*

give *a reason for the hope that is in you* (1 Peter 3:15)? If I were to ask those who are really Christians here to rise, would you be ashamed to stand up? Suppose I asked every professed child of God here, "If you were cut down by the hand of death, do you have good reason to believe you would be saved?" Would you be willing to stand up before God and man and say that you have good reason to believe you are *passed from death into life* (John 5:24)? Or would you be ashamed?

Run your mind back over the past years: would your life and actions correspond with your profession of faith? It is not what we say so much as how we live. Actions speak louder than words. Do your coworkers know that you are a Christian? Does your family know? Do they know you to be out and out on the Lord's side? Let every professed Christian ask, "Where am I in the sight of God? Is my heart loyal to the King of heaven? Is my life here as it should be in the community I live in? Am I a light in this dark world?" Christ calls us His witnesses. Christ was the Light of the world, and the world did not want the true

Light. The world rose up and put out the Light, and now Christ says, "I leave *you* down here to testify of Me; I leave you down here as My witnesses" (Acts 1:8). That is what the Apostle meant when he said that Christians are to be living epistles, *known and read by all men* (2 Corinthians 3:2). Am I standing up for Jesus as I should in this dark world? If a man is for God, let him say so. If a man is for God, let him openly be on God's side; and if he is for the world, let him be in the world. This serving God and the world at the same time – this being on both sides at the same time – is just the curse of Christianity at the present time. It slows the progress of Christianity more than any other thing. *"If anyone desires to come after Me, let him deny himself, and take up his cross daily, and follow Me"* (Luke 9:23).

I have heard of many people who think if they join a church and make a profession of faith, that will do for the rest of their days. But there is a cross for every one of us *daily*. O child of God, where are you? If God would appear to you tonight and ask the question, "Where are you?" what would your answer be? Could you say, "Lord, I am serving You with my whole heart and strength; I am improving my talents and preparing for the kingdom to come"?

When I was in England in 1867, there was a merchant who came over from Dublin and was talking with a businessman in London. As I happened to look in, he introduced me to the man from Dublin. Alluding to me, the latter said to the former, "Is this young man an 'O O'?"

The London man asked, "What do you mean by 'O O'?"

The Dublin man replied, "Is he 'Out-and-Out' for Christ?"

That burned down into my soul. It means a good deal to be 'O O' for Christ, but that is what all Christians ought to be. If people who are on the Lord's side would take their stand and lift up their voices in season and out of season, their influence would be felt on the world very soon.

As I have said, there are many in the church who once made a profession, and that is about all you hear of them. When they die, you have to go hunt through some musty old church records to know whether they were Christians or not. God will not do that. I have an idea that when Daniel died, all the men in Babylon knew whom he served. There was no need for them to hunt through old books. His life told his story. What we want is people with a little courage to stand up for Christ. When Christianity wakes up and every child that belongs to the Lord is willing to speak for Him, is willing to work for Him, and, if need be, willing to die for Him, then Christianity will advance, and we will see the work of the Lord prosper. There is one thing that I fear more than anything else, and that is the dead, cold formalism of the church of God. Talk about the *isms*! Even taken all together, I do not fear them so much as dead, cold formalism. Talk about the *false isms!* There is none so dangerous as this dead, cold formalism that has come right into the heart of the church. There are so many of us just slumbering and sleeping while souls all around are perishing. I believe honestly that we professed Christians are all half-asleep. Some of us are beginning to rub our eyes and get them half-opened, but as a whole, we are asleep.

There was a story making the rounds of the American press that made a great impression on me as a father. A father took his little child out into the field one Sunday, and it being a hot day, he lay down under a beautiful shady tree. The little boy ran around gathering wildflowers and little blades of grass and brought them to his father, saying, "Pretty! Pretty!" At last, the father fell asleep, and while he was sleeping, the little child wandered away. When he awoke, his first thought was, "Where is my son?" He looked all around, but he could not see him. He shouted at the top of his voice, but all he heard was the echo of his own voice. Running to a little hill, he looked around and shouted again. No response! Then going to a precipice at some distance, he looked down, and there, on the rocks and briars, he saw the mangled form of his loved child. He rushed to the spot, picked up the lifeless corpse, hugged it to his chest, and accused himself of being the murderer of his child. While he was sleeping, his son had wandered over the precipice. As I heard that, I thought *what a picture of the church of God!*

How many fathers and mothers, how many Christian men, are sleeping now while their children wander over the terrible precipice right into the bottomless pit of hell. Dad, where is your boy tonight? He may be just out there in some bar; he may be reeling through the streets; he may be pressing on to a drunkard's grave. Mom, where is your son? Is he drinking away his soul – everything that is dear and sacred to him? Do you know where your boy is? Dad, you have been a professed Christian for forty years; where are your children tonight? Have you lived so godly and so Christlike that you can say, "Follow me as I followed Christ"? Are those children walking in wisdom? Are they on their way to glory? Have they been gathered into the fold of Christ? Are their names written in the Lamb's Book of Life? How many fathers and mothers today would be able to answer? Did you ever stop to think that you were to blame, that you had not been faithful to your children? Count on it, as long as the church is living so much like the world, we cannot expect our children to be brought into the fold. Come, O Lord, and wake up every mother. And may every one of us who are parents feel the worth of the souls of the children whom God has given us. May they never bring our gray hairs to the grave with sorrow, but may they become a blessing to the church and to the world.

Not long ago the only daughter of a wealthy man I knew became sick and died. The father and mother stood by her deathbed. He had spent all his time accumulating wealth for her, and she had been introduced into fashionable society; but she had been taught nothing of Christ. As she came to the brink of the river of death, she said, "Won't you help me? It is very dark, and the stream is bitter cold." They wrung their hands in grief but could do nothing for her; and the poor girl died in darkness and despair. What was their wealth to them then? Yet you mothers and fathers are doing the same thing today by ignoring the work God has given you to do. I beg you, then, each one of you, begin to work now for the souls of your children!

Some time ago, a young man lay dying, and his mother thought he was a Christian. One day, passing the door to his room, she heard him say, "Lost! Lost! Lost!"

The mother ran into the room and cried, "My boy, is it possible you have lost your hope in Christ now that you are dying?"

"No, mother, it is not that. I have hope beyond the grave, but I have lost my life. I have lived twenty-four years and done nothing for the Son of God, and now I am dying. My life has been spent for myself. I have lived for this world, and now, while I am dying, I have given myself to Christ, but my life is lost." Would it not be said of many of us, if we were to die, that our lives have been almost a failure – perhaps entirely a failure, as far as leading anyone else to Christ is concerned? Young lady, are you working for the Son of God? Are you trying to win some soul to Christ? Have you tried to get a friend or companion to have her name written in the Book of Life? Or would you say, "Lost, lost! Long years have passed since I became a child of God, and I have never had the privilege of leading one soul to Christ"? If there is one professed child of God who never had the joy of leading even one soul into the kingdom of God, oh, let him begin at once. There is no greater privilege on earth. And I believe, my friends, there has never been a time, in our day, at least, when work for Christ was more needed than now.

I do not believe there ever was in your day or mine a time when the Spirit of God was more poured out on the world. There is not a part of Christendom where the work is not being carried on, and it looks very much as if the glad tidings are going to continue around the globe. It is time that the people of the church of God wake up and come together for the work of the Lord and strive to beat back those dark waves of death that roll through our streets, bearing the noblest and the best we have. Oh, may God wake up the church! Let your light burn brighter, and go out to work for the kingdom of His Son.

Second, let me talk a little while to those who have gone back into the world – to backsliders. Perhaps you were a professed Christian when you moved to the city a few years ago. You were a member of a church once and maybe even a Sunday school teacher, but when you were among strangers, you thought you would wait just a little while before attending a class. So you gave up teaching in Sunday school; you gave up all work for Christ. Then because you did not receive the attention or the warm welcome that you expected in your new church, you got into the habit of staying away. And now you have stayed away so long that you can be found in places you should not be and are the companion of blasphemers and drunks.

Perhaps I am speaking now to someone who has been away from his father's house for many years. Tell me, backslider, are you happy? Have you had one happy hour since you left Christ? Does the world or those pods you shared with the pigs in the far country satisfy you? (Luke 15:16). I have traveled a lot, but I never found a happy backslider in my life. I never knew a person who was really born of God that found the world could satisfy him afterward. Do you think the Prodigal Son was satisfied in that foreign country? Ask the prodigals in this city if they are truly happy. You know they are not. *"There is no peace,"* says the LORD, *"for the wicked"* (Isaiah 48:22). There is no joy for the man in rebellion against his Creator. If he has tasted the heavenly gift, been in communion with God, had sweet fellowship with the King of Heaven, and had pleasant hours of service for the Master but has backslidden, is it possible that he can be happy? If he is, it is good evidence that he was never really converted. If a man has been born again and has received the heavenly nature, this world can never satisfy the cravings of his nature.

O backslider, I pity you! But I want to tell you that the Lord Jesus pities you more than anyone else can. He knows how bitter your life is. He knows how dark your life is, and He wants you to come home. Backslider, come home tonight! I have a loving message from your Father. The Lord wants you and calls you back tonight, "Come home, O wanderer, this night. Return from the dark mountains of sin." Return, and your Father will give you a warm welcome. I know that the devil has told you that God won't have anything to do with you because you have wandered away. If that is true, there would be very few men in heaven. David backslid; Abraham and Jacob turned away from God. I do not believe there is a saint in heaven that at some time of his life has not with his heart backslidden from God. Perhaps not in his life but in his heart. The prodigal's heart went to the far country before his body got there. Backslider, come home tonight. Your Father does not want you to stay away. Do you think the prodigal's father was not anxious for him to come home all those long years he was there? Every year the father was looking and longing for him to return home. So God wants you to come home. I do not care how far you have wandered away; the great Shepherd will receive you back into the fold tonight. Did you ever hear of a backslider coming home and God not willing to receive him? I have heard of earthly fathers and mothers not being willing to receive their children, but I defy any man to say he ever knew an honest backslider want to get home who found God unwilling to take him in.

Several years ago, before any railway came into Chicago, they used to bring in the grain from the Western prairies in wagons for hundreds of miles so it could be shipped off by the Great Lakes. There was a father who had a large farm out there who used to preach the gospel as well as attend to his farm. One day, when church business engaged him, he sent his son to Chicago with grain. He waited and waited for his boy to return, but he did not come home. At last, he could wait no longer, so he saddled his horse and rode to the place where his son had sold the grain. He found that he had been there and received the money for the grain, so he began to fear that his boy had been murdered and robbed. At last, with the aid of a detective, they tracked him to a gambling hall, where they found that he had gambled away all his money. In hopes of winning it back, he then had sold the horses and lost that money too. He had fallen among thieves, and like the man who was going to Jericho, they stripped him, and then they cared no more about him. What could he do? He was ashamed to go home to meet his father, and he fled. The father knew what it all meant. He knew the boy thought he would be very angry with him. He was grieved to think that his boy would have such feelings toward him. That is exactly like the sinner. He thinks because he has sinned, God will have nothing to do with him.

But what did that father do? Did he say, "Let the boy go"? No; he went after him. He arranged his business and started after the boy. That man went from town to town, from city to city. He would get the ministers to let him preach, and at the close, he would tell his story. "I have a son who is a wanderer on the face of the earth somewhere." He would describe his boy and say, "If you ever hear of him or see him, will you not write to me?" At last, he found that he had gone to California, thousands of miles away. Did that father say, "Let him go!"? No. Off he went to the Pacific coast, looking for the boy. He went to San Francisco and advertised in the newspapers that he would preach at such a church on such a day. When he had preached, he told his story in hopes that the boy might have seen the advertisement and come to the church. When he had finished, back under the balcony, there was a young man who waited until the audience had gone out; then he came toward the pulpit. The father looked and saw it was his son, and he ran to him and held him to his chest. The boy wanted to confess what he had done, but the father would not hear a word. He forgave him freely and took him home once more.

Oh, prodigal, you may be wandering on the dark mountains of sin, but God wants you to come home. The devil has been telling you lies about God; you think He will not take you back, but He will welcome you this minute if you come. Say, *"I will arise and go to my father"* (Luke 15:18). May God incline you to take this step.

*O backslider, come home to your Father's house.*

There is not one whom Jesus has not sought far longer than that father. There has not been a day since you left Him that He has not followed you. I do not care what the past has been or how black your life is, He will receive you. O backslider, come home to your Father's house.

Not long ago, in Edinburgh, a lady who was an earnest Christian worker, found a young woman whose feet had taken hold of hell and who was heading to a harlot's grave. The lady begged her to go back to her home, but she said no; her parents would never receive her. This Christian woman knew what a mother's heart was, so she sat down and wrote a letter to the mother, telling her how she had met her daughter, who was sorry and wanted to return. The next post brought an answer back, and on the envelope was written, "Immediately – immediately!" That was a mother's heart. They opened the letter. Yes, she was forgiven. They wanted her back, and they sent money for her to come *immediately*. Sinner, that is the proclamation, "Come *immediately*." That is what the great and loving God is saying to every wandering sinner – *immediately*. Yes, backslider, come home tonight. He will give you a warm welcome, and there will be joy in heaven over your return. Come now, because everything is ready.

A friend of mine said to me some time ago, "Did you ever notice what the prodigal lost by going into that far country?" First, he lost his *food*. That is what all the poor backsliders lose. They get no manna from heaven. The Bible is a closed book to them; they see no beauty in the Word of God.

Then the prodigal lost his *work*. He was a Jew, and they made him take care of pigs; that was all loss for a Jew. And every backslider loses his work. He cannot do anything for God; he cannot work for eternity. He is a stumbling block to the world. My friend, do not let the world stumble over you into hell.

The prodigal also lost his *testimony*. Who believed him? I can imagine some men of that country came along and saw this poor prodigal in his rags, barefooted and bareheaded. There he stood among the pigs, and someone said to another, "Look at that poor wretch."

He replied, "Why do you call me a poor wretch? My father is a wealthy man; he has more clothes in his closet than you ever saw in your life. My father is a man of great wealth and position." Do you suppose those men would believe him?

"That poor wretch, the son of a wealthy man?" Not one of them would believe him. "If he had such a wealthy father, he would go to him." So it is with the backsliders; the world does not believe that they are the sons of a King. They say, "Why don't they go to Him if there is bread enough to spare? Why don't they go home?"

Another thing the prodigal lost was his *home*. He had no home in that foreign country. As long as his money lasted, he was quite popular in the bars and among his acquaintances. People claimed to be his friends, but as soon as his money was gone, where were they? That is the condition of every poor backslider here.

But now I can imagine someone saying, "There is no use of my attempting to go back. In a few days, I would just end up back where I was. I want to go to my Father's house again, but I am afraid I would not stay there." Well, picture this scene. The poor prodigal has gone home, and the father has killed the fatted calf. There they are, sitting at the table eating. I can imagine that was about the sweetest food he ever tasted – perhaps the nicest dinner he ever had in his life. His father sits opposite him; he is full of joy, and his heart is leaping within him. All at once, he sees his boy weeping. "My son, why are you weeping? Are you not glad to be home?"

"Oh, yes, father; I never was so glad as I am today, but I am so afraid I will go back to that foreign country!" Why, you cannot imagine such a thing! When you have had one meal in your Father's house, you will never be inclined to wander away again.

Now let me speak to the third class of people. *"If the righteous one is scarcely saved, where will the ungodly and the sinner appear?"* (1 Peter 4:18). Sinner, what is to become of you? How will you escape? *"Where are you?"* Is it true that you are living without God and without hope in the world? Did you ever stop to think what would become of your soul if you would be taken away by a sudden stroke of illness – where you would stand in eternity? I read that the sinner is without God, without hope, and without excuse (Ephesians 2:12; Romans 1:20). If you are not saved, what excuse will you have to give? You cannot say that it is God's fault. He is anxious to save you. I want to tell you tonight that you can be saved if you want to be. If you really want to pass from death to life, if you want to become an heir of eternal life, if you want to become a child of God, make up your mind this night that you will seek the kingdom of God. I tell you on the authority of this Word, if you seek the kingdom of God, you will find it. No person with his heart set to find Christ ever looked for Him without finding Him. I never knew anyone make up his mind to have the question settled who did not have it settled quickly.

This last year there has been a solemn feeling stealing over me. I am what they call in the middle of life, in the prime of life. I look on life as a man who has reached the top of a hill and is just beginning to go down the other side. I have gotten to the top of the hill, if I should live the full term of life – seventy years – and am just on the other side. I am speaking to many now who are also on the top of the hill, and if you are not Christians, I ask you to pause a few minutes and ask yourselves where you are. Look back on the hill that we have been climbing. What do you see? There is the cradle. It is not far away. How short life is! It all seems like yesterday. Look up the hill, and there is a tombstone; it marks the resting place of a loved mother. When that mother died, did you not promise God that you would serve Him? Did you not say that your mother's God would become your God? And did you not take her hand in the stillness of her dying hour, and say, "Yes, mother, I will meet you in heaven!" Have you kept that promise? Are you trying to keep it? Ten years have rolled away, fifteen years – but are you any nearer to God? Did the promise work any improvement in you? No, your heart is getting harder. The night is getting darker, and soon death will be throwing its shadows around you. My friend, where are you?

Look again. A little further up the hill there is another tombstone. It marks the resting place of a little child. It may have been a lovely little girl – perhaps her name was Mary; or it may have been a boy – Charley. When that child was taken from you, did you not promise God, and did you not promise the child that you would meet your darling in heaven? Is the promise kept? Think! Are you still fighting against God? Are you still hardening your heart? Sermons that would have moved you five years ago – do they touch you now?

Once more look down the hill. Down there is a grave; you cannot tell how many days or weeks or years it is away; you are hurrying toward that grave. Even if you live the life allotted to man, many of you are near the end. You are getting very feeble, and your hair is turning gray. It may be that already the decree has gone out. It may be that your coffin is already waiting. My friend, is it not the height of madness to put off salvation so long? Undoubtedly, I am speaking to some who will be in eternity a week from now. In a large audi- *Will there ever be a better opportunity?* ence like this, during the next week death will surely come and snatch some away. It may be the speaker, or it may be someone who is reading this now. Why put off the question another day? Why say to the Lord Jesus again tonight, "Go away for now. When it is more convenient for me, I will call for You"? Why not let Him come in tonight? Open your heart and say, "King of Glory, come in!"

Will there ever be a better opportunity? Did you not promise ten, fifteen, twenty, thirty years ago that you would serve God? Some of you said you would do it when you got married and settled down; some of you said you would serve Him when you were your own boss. Have you done it?

There are three steps down to the world of the lost; let me give you their names. The first step is *Neglect*. All a man has to do is to neglect salvation, and that will take him to the lost world. Some people say, "What have I done? Why am I here?" Why, if you merely neglect salvation, you will be lost. I am on a swift river, lying in the bottom of my little boat. Ten miles below is the great waterfall. Everyone who goes over it dies. I do not need to row the boat down to die; I only have to pull in the oars, fold my arms, and *neglect*. All that a man has to do is to fold his arms in the current of life, and he will drift onward and be lost.

The second step is *Refusal*. If I met you at the door and asked you this question about your salvation, you would say, "Not tonight, Mr. Moody, not tonight." And if I repeated, "I want you to embrace the kingdom of God," you would politely refuse: "I will not become a Christian tonight, thank you. I know I ought to, but I *won't* tonight."

Then the last step is to *Despise* it. Some of you are already on the lowest rung of the ladder. You despise Christ. You hate Christ, you hate Christianity. You hate the best people on earth and the best friends you have, and if I were to offer you the Bible, you would tear it up and put your foot on it. Oh, despisers! You will soon be in another world. Quickly, repent and turn to God.

Which step are you on, my friend? Neglecting, refusing, or despising? Keep in mind that many are taken off from the first step: they die in neglect. Many are taken away refusing. And many are on the last step, despising salvation.

A few years ago, they *neglected*. Then they began to *refuse,* and now they *despise* Christianity and Christ. They hate the sound of the church bell. They hate the Bible and the Christian; they curse the very ground that we walk on. But one more step, and they are gone. O despisers, I set before you life and death; which will you choose? When Pilate had Christ on his hands, he said, *"What then do you want me to do with Him?"* (Mark 15:12), and the multitude cried out, *"Away with Him! Crucify Him!"* (John 19:15). Young people, is that your language tonight? Do you say, "Away with this gospel! Away with Christianity! Away with your prayers, your sermons, your gospel! I do not want Christ"? Or will you be wise and say, "Lord Jesus, I want You, I need You, I will have You"? May God bring you to that decision!

# THERE IS NO DIFFERENCE

*For there is no difference; for all have*
*sinned and fall short of the glory of God.*
– Romans 3:22-23

This is one of the hardest truths we have to learn. We are apt to think that we are just a little better than our neighbors, and if we find they are a little better than ourselves, we go to work to try to pull them down to our level. If you want to find out who and what man is, go to Romans 3, and there the whole story is told. *"There is none righteous, no, not one"* (Romans 3:10) and *All have sinned and fall short* (Romans 3:23). *All.* Some men like to have their lives written before they die; if any of you would like to read your biography, turn to this chapter, and you will find it already recorded.

I can imagine someone saying, "I wonder if he really pretends to say that *there is no difference*" (Romans 3:22). The teetotaler says, "Am I no better than the drunk?" Well, I want to say right here that it is better to be a teetotaler than a drunk; better to be honest than dishonest. It is better for a man to be upright in all his transactions than to cheat right and left, even in this life. But when it comes to the great question of salvation, that does not touch the question at all because *all have sinned and fall short of the glory of God*. Men are all bad by nature; the old Adam stock is bad, and we cannot bring forth good fruit until we are grafted into the one True Vine. If I have an orchard with two apple trees in it and both bear perfectly worthless bitter apples, does it make any difference to me that the one tree has perhaps five hundred bad apples and the other only two, both bad? There is no difference; only one tree has more fruit than the other. But it is all *bad*.

It is the same with us. One thinks he has only one or two very little sins – God won't notice that; why, that other man has broken every one of the Ten Commandments! It does not matter, there is no difference. They are both guilty; they have both broken the law. The law demands complete and perfect fulfillment, and if you cannot do that, you are lost as far as the law is concerned. *Whoever shall keep the whole law, and yet stumble in one point, he is guilty of all* (James 2:10). Suppose you were to hang a man from the roof with a chain of ten links; if one were to break, does it matter that the other nine are all sound and whole? Not in the least. If one link breaks, down comes the man. But is it not rather harsh that he should fall when only one is broken and the other nine are perfect? Why, of course not. If one is broken, it is just the same to the man as if they all had broken. He falls. So the person who breaks one commandment is guilty of all. He is a criminal in God's sight. Look at that prison over there with its thousand victims. Some are there for murder, some for stealing, some for forgery, some for one thing, and some for another. You may classify them, but every man is a *criminal*. They have all broken the law, and they are all paying the penalty. The law has made every man a criminal in the sight of God.

If a man would advertise that he could take an accurate

photograph of people's hearts, do you believe he would find a customer? There is not a man among us whom you could persuade to have his photograph taken if you could photograph *the real man*. We go to have our portraits taken and carefully arrange our clothes and hair; and if the artist flatters us, we say, "Oh, yes, that's a first-rate likeness," as we show it to our friends. But if the real man could be seen, if you could take a photograph of the heart, see if a man will pass that around among his neighbors. Why, you would not want your own spouse to see it! You would be frightened even to look at it yourself. Nobody knows what is in that heart but Christ.

We are told *"the heart is deceitful above all things, and desperately wicked; who can know it?"* (Jeremiah 17:9). We do not know our own hearts; none of us have any idea how bad they are. Some bitter things are written against me, but I know many more things about myself that are bad than any other man does. There is nothing good in the old Adam nature. We have a heart in rebellion against God by nature, and we do not even love God unless we are born of the Spirit. I *We do not know our own hearts.* can understand why men do not like Romans 3 – it is too strong for them. It speaks the truth too plainly. But just because we do not like it, we will be better off if we look at it. Very likely we will find that it is exactly what we need. It's a truth that men do not like at all, but I have noticed that the medicine we do not like is the medicine that will do us the most good. If we do not think we are as bad as the description, we must take a closer look at ourselves.

Perhaps there is one here who thinks he is not quite so bad as the Scriptures make him out to be. He is sure he is a little better than his neighbor next door; why, he goes to church regularly, and his neighbor never goes to church at all! "Of course," he congratulates himself, "I am nearer to salvation than he is." But there is no use trying to evade it. God has given us the law to measure ourselves by, and by this most perfect rule, we have all sinned and fallen short, and *there is no difference.*

Paul brings in the law to show man that he is lost and ruined. God, being a perfect God, had to give a perfect law, and the law was given not to save men but to measure them by. I want you to understand this clearly because I believe hundreds and thousands stumble here. They try to save themselves by trying to keep the law; but it was never meant for men to save themselves by. The law has never saved a single person since the world began. People have been trying to keep it, but they have never succeeded and never will. Ask Paul what it was given for. Here is his answer: *That every mouth may be stopped, and all the world may become guilty before God* (Romans 3:19). In this chapter of Romans, the world has been put on trial and found guilty. The verdict has been brought in against us all – ministers and elders and church members, just as much as the prodigal and the drunk. All have sinned and fallen short.

The law shuts every man's mouth. God wants a man to humble himself down on his face before Him, with not a word to say for himself. Then God will speak to him when he admits that he is a sinner and gets rid of all his own righteousness. I can always tell a man who has gone near the kingdom of God: his mouth is closed. If you will allow me the expression, God always shuts a man's lips before He saves him.

Job was not delivered until he stopped talking about himself. See how God dealt with him. First, He afflicted him, and Job began to talk about his own goodness. *I delivered the poor who cried out, the fatherless and the one who had no helper. . . I was eyes to the blind, and I was feet to the lame. I was a father to the poor* (Job 29:12, 15-16). They would have made Job an elder if there had been elders in those days! He had been a wonderfully good man! But then God said, *"Now prepare yourself like a man; I will question you, and you shall answer Me"* (Job 38:3). Job was quickly humbled; he was ashamed of himself. He could not speak of his works anymore. *"Behold,"* he cried, *"I am vile; what shall I answer You? I lay my hand over my mouth"* (Job 40:4). But he was not low enough yet, perhaps, and God asked a few more questions. Job said, "I never understood these things before – I never saw it in that light." He was thoroughly humbled now; he can't help confessing it. *"I have heard of You by the hearing of the ear, but now my eye sees You. Therefore I abhor myself, and repent in dust and ashes"* (Job 42:5-6). Now he had found his right position before God, and now God could talk to him. God helped him, raised him up, and gave him double of all that he had before. The clouds, the mist, and the darkness around his path were driven away, and light from eternity burst into his soul when he saw his nothingness in the sight of a pure and holy God.

This, then, is what God gives us the law for – to show us ourselves in our true colors.

One morning, a few weeks before the Chicago fire, I said to my little family, "I am coming home this afternoon to give you a ride." My little boy clapped his hands.

"Oh, Papa, will you take me to see the bears in Lincoln Park?"

"Yes." You know boys are very fond of seeing bears. I had not been gone long when my little boy said, "Mamma, I wish you would get me ready."

"Oh," she said, "it will be a long time before Papa comes."

"But I want to get ready, Mamma." At last, he was ready: his face washed and clothes all nice and clean.

"Now, you must take good care and not get yourself dirty again," said Mamma.

Oh, of course he was going to take care; he wasn't going to get dirty. So off he ran to watch for me. However, it was still a long time until the afternoon, and after a little while, he began to play. When I got home, I found him outside, his face all covered with dirt.

"I can't take you to the park that way, Willie."

"Why, Papa? You said you would take me."

"Ah, but I can't; you're all covered with mud. I couldn't be seen with such a dirty little boy."

"Why, I'm clean, Papa; Mamma washed me."

"Well, you've gotten dirty since." But he began to cry, and I could not convince him that he was dirty.

"I'm clean; Mamma washed me!" he cried. Do you think I argued with him? No. I just took him up in my arms and carried him into the house and showed him his face in the mirror. He did not have a word to say. He could not take my word for it, but one look in the mirror was enough; he saw it for himself. He didn't say he wasn't dirty after that!

Now the mirror showed him that his face was dirty – but I did not use the mirror to wash it; of course not. Yet that is what thousands of people do. The law is the mirror to see ourselves in, to show us how vile and worthless we are in the sight of God, but men take the law and try to wash themselves with it!

*The law is the mirror to see ourselves in.*

Man has been trying that for thousands of years and has miserably failed. *By the deeds of the law no flesh will be justified in His sight* (Romans 3:20). Only one Man ever lived on the earth who could say He had kept the law, and that was the Lord Jesus Christ. If He had committed one sin and come short in the smallest degree, His offering Himself for us would have been useless. But men have tried to do what He did and have failed. Instead of sheltering under His righteousness, they have offered God their own. And God knew what a miserable failure it would be. *"There is none righteous, no, not one."*

I don't care where you put man, everywhere he has been tried, he has proved a total failure. He was put in Eden on trial – some men say they wish they had Adam's chance. If you had, you would go down as quickly as he did. Put five hundred children into this hall and give them ten thousand toys. Tell them they can run all over the hall, and they can have anything they want except one thing, placed, let us say, in one of the corners of Mr. Sankey's organ.[1] If you go out for a little, do you not think that is the very first place they will go to? Why, nothing else in the room would have any attraction for them except the thing they were told not to touch. So we should not think Adam was any worse than we are. Adam was put on trial, and Satan walked into Eden. I do not know how long he was there, but I would guess he had not been there twenty minutes before he stripped Adam of everything he had. There was Adam, fresh from the hands of his Creator; Satan comes on the scene and presents a temptation, and down he goes. *He was a failure.*

Then God took man into covenant with Him. He said to Abraham, "Look at the stars in the heavens and the sands on the seashore; I will make your seed like that. I will bless you and multiply you on the earth" (Genesis 15). But what a stupendous failure man was under the covenant! Go back and read about it.

They were brought out of Egypt, saw many signs and wonders, and stood at last at the foot of Mount Sinai. Then God's holy law was given to them. Did they not promise to keep it? "Oh yes," they cried, "we'll keep the law, certainly!" To hear them talk, you might think it was going to be all right now. But as soon as Moses and Joshua turned their backs, as soon as their leader had gone up the mountain to have an interview with God, they began saying, "Wonder what's become of this man Moses? We don't know where he's gone. Come, let us make us another god. Aaron, make us a golden calf. Here are the golden ornaments we got from the Egyptians; come make us another god."

---

1    Ira Sankey (1840-1908) was an American singer and composer who traveled with Dwight Moody and led the music in his evangelistic meetings.

So when it was made, the people raised a great shout and fell down and worshipped it. "Listen! What is that sound that I hear?" said Moses as he came down the mountainside.

Joshua answered, "There's war in the camp. It is the shout of the victor."

"No," replied Moses, "it isn't the shout of victory or of war, Joshua. It is the cry of the idolaters. They have forgotten the God who delivered them from the Egyptians, who led them through the Red Sea, who fed them with bread from heaven – angels' food. They have forgotten their promises to keep the commandments. Already the first two of them are broken: no other gods, no carved images (Exodus 20:3-4). They've made themselves another god – a golden god!" And that's what men have been doing ever since.

There are more men in England worshipping the golden calf than the God of heaven. Look around you. They bring before it health and happiness and peace. "Give me thirty pieces of silver, and I will sell you Christ," is the world's cry today. "Give me fashion, and I will sell you Christ!" "I will sacrifice my wife, my children, my life, my all, for a little drink. I will sell my soul for pleasure!" It is easy to blame these men for worshipping the golden calf. But what are we doing? Man was a failure then, and he has been a failure ever since.

Then God put him under the judges. They were wonderful judges, but, once more, what a failure man was! After that came the prophets, and what a failure he was under them! Then came the Son Himself from heaven, right out of the bosom of the Father. He left the throne and came down here to teach us how to live. We took Him and murdered Him on Calvary! Man was a failure in Christ's time.

Now we are living under the dispensation of grace – a wonderful dispensation. God is showering down blessings from above. But what is man under grace? A stupendous failure.

Look at that man reeling on his way to an alcoholic's grave and his soul to hell. Look at the harlots on your streets. Look at the evil and the poverty and the loathsome sickness. If you look at the vice and crime that fester everywhere, you cannot tell me that man is not a failure under grace.

Yes, man is a failure. Even if I could look ahead to the time of the millennium. Christ will sway His scepter over the earth for a thousand years, but man will still be a failure. For *when the thousand years have expired, Satan will be released from his prison and will go out to deceive the nations which are in the four corners of the earth, Gog and Magog, to gather them together to battle... and surrounded the camp of the saints and the beloved city. And fire came down from God out of heaven and devoured them* (Revelation 20:7-9). What man needs is another nature; he must be born again. What a foolish saying, "Experience teaches." Man has been a long time at that school and has still not learned his lesson – his own weakness and inability. He still thinks great things of his own strength. "I am going to stand after this," he says. "I have hit on the right plan this time. I am able to keep the law now." But the first temptation comes, and he is down. Man will not believe in God's strength. Man will not acknowledge that he is a failure and surrender to Christ to save him from his sins. But it is better to find out in this world that we are a failure and to go to Christ for deliverance than to sleep on and go down to hell without ever knowing we are sinners.

I know this doctrine that we have all failed, that we have all sinned and come short, is very objectionable to the natural man. If I had tried to discover the most disagreeable verse in the whole Bible, perhaps I could not have found one more universally disliked than *"There is no difference."*

I can imagine – and I think I have a right to imagine it – Noah leaving his ark and going around preaching occasionally. As people stop to listen, there is no sound of the hammer or the

saw. Noah has stopped working. He has gone off on a preaching tour to warn his countrymen. Perhaps he told them that
there was a great deluge coming to sweep away all the workers
of iniquity; perhaps he warned them that *every* man who was
not in the ark would perish, that there would be *no difference.*
I can imagine one man saying, "You had better go back and
finish your work, Noah, rather than come here preaching. You
don't think we are going to believe in such nonsense as that. You
tell us that all are going to perish alike! Do you really expect
us to believe that the kings and governors, the sheriffs and the
princes, the rulers, the beggars and thieves and harlots are all
going to be identically lost?"

"Yes," said Noah. "The deluge that is coming will take you
all away – every person who is not in the ark will die. There
will be no difference." Undoubtedly, they thought Noah had
gone raving mad. But the flood did come and take them all
away. Princes and paupers, knaves and kings – was there any
difference? No difference.

When the destroying angel was about to pass through Egypt,
no doubt the haughty Egyptian laughed at the poor Israelite
putting the blood on his doorpost and lintel. "What a foolish
notion," he would say derisively; "the very idea of sprinkling
blood on a doorpost! If there *were* anything coming, that would
never keep it away. I don't believe there is any death coming at
all, and if it did, it might touch these poor people, but it would
certainly never come near us." But when the night came, there
was no difference. The king in his palace, the captive in his
prison, the beggar by the wayside – they were all alike. Into
every house the king of terrors had come, and there was universal mourning in the land. In the home of the poor and the
lowly, in the home of the prince and the noble, in the home of
the governor and ruler, the eldest son lay dead. Only the poor
Israelite escaped who had the blood on the doorpost and lintel.

And when God comes to us in judgment, if we are not in Christ, all will be alike. Educated or uneducated, rich or poor, priest or scribe – there will be no difference.

Once more, I can imagine Abraham going down from the hills to Sodom. He stood up, let us say, at the corners of the streets, before Sodom was destroyed. "You men of Sodom, I have a message from my God to you." The people stood and looked at the old man – you can see his white hair as the wind sweeps through it. "I have a warning for you," he cried. "God is going to destroy the five cities of the plain, and every man who does not escape to the mountains will per-

*Educated or uneducated, rich or poor, priest or scribe – there will be no difference.*

ish. When He comes to deal in judgment with you, there will be no difference; every person must die. The mayor, the princes, the chief men, the mighty men, the judges, the treasurers – all must die. The thief, the vagabond, and the drunk – yes, all must perish alike. There can be no difference."

But these Sodomites answered, "You had better go back to your tent on the hills, Abraham. We don't believe a word of it. Sodom was never so prosperous, business was never so flourishing as now. The sun never shone any brighter than it does today. The lambs are skipping on the hills, and everything is moving on as it has done for centuries. Don't preach that stuff to us; we don't believe it." A few hours passed, and Sodom was in ashes! Did God make any difference among those who would not believe? No, God never utters any opinion; what He says is truth. He cries, "All have sinned and fallen short and there is no difference." The Bible speaks of a deluge of fire that is going to roll over this earth (2 Peter 3:12), and when God comes to deal in judgment, there will be no difference. Every man who is not in Christ will perish.

It was my sad experience to be in the Chicago fire. As the

flames rolled down our streets, destroying everything in their onward march, I saw the great and the honorable, the educated and the wise, fleeing from the fire with the beggar, the thief, and the harlot. All were alike. As the flames swept through the city, it was like judgment day. Neither the mayor nor the mighty men nor the wise men could stop these flames. They were all on level ground then, and many who were worth millions were left paupers that night.

When the day of judgment comes, there will be no difference. When the deluge came, there was no difference; Noah's ark was worth more than all the world. The day before it was the world's laughingstock, and if it had been put up for auction, you could not have gotten anyone to buy it except for firewood. But the deluge came, and then it was worth more than all the world put together. And when the day of judgment comes, Christ will be worth more than all this world, more than ten thousand worlds. If it was a terrible thing in the days of Noah to die outside the ark, it will be far more terrible for us to go down in our sins to a Christless grave.

Now I hope that you have seen what I have been trying to prove – that we are all sinners alike. If I have failed to prove that, then the meeting tonight has been a failure. I would like to use another illustration or two. I would like to make this truth so plain that a child might know it. In England, a long time ago, they used to have a game of firing arrows through a ring on the top of a pole. The man who failed to get all his arrows through the ring was called a *sinner*. Now I would like for a moment to talk about that illustration. Suppose our pole is up on the balcony and on top of it the ring. I have ten arrows, and Mr. Sankey has another ten. I pick up the first arrow and take good aim, but I miss the mark. Therefore, I am a *sinner*. But I say to myself, "I will do the best I can with the other nine; I have only missed with one." Like some men who try to keep all the commandments except one! I fire again and miss the mark a second time. "Ah," I say, "I still have eight arrows," and away goes another arrow – a miss! I fire all ten arrows and do not get one through the ring. Well, I was a sinner after the first miss, and I can only be a sinner after the tenth.

Now Mr. Sankey comes with his ten arrows. He fires and gets his first arrow through. "Do you see that?" he says.

"Well," I reply, "go on; don't boast until you get them all through." He takes the second arrow and gets that through.

"Ha! do you see that?"

"Don't boast," I repeat, "until all ten are through." If a man has not broken the law at all then he does have something to boast of! Away goes the third, and it goes through. Then another and another and another until nine are through.

"Now," he says, "one more arrow, and I am not a sinner." He picks up the last arrow, and his hand trembles a little; he *just misses* the mark. *And he is a sinner just as much as I am.* My friend, have you never missed the mark? Have you not come short? I would like to see the man who never missed the mark. He never lived.

Let me give you just one more illustration. When Chicago was a small town, it was incorporated and made a city. When we got our charter for the city, there was one clause in the constitution that allowed the mayor to appoint all the police. It worked very well when it was a small city, but when it had three or four hundred thousand inhabitants, it put too much power in the hands of one man. So our leading citizens got a new bill passed that took the power out of the hands of the mayor and put it into the hands of commissioners appointed by government. One clause in the new law stated that no man could be a policeman who was not a certain height – five feet six inches, let us say. When the commissioners got into power, they advertised for men as candidates, and in the advertisement, they stated that no man need apply who could not bring good credentials to recommend him.

I remember going past the office one day, and there was a crowd of people waiting to get in. They blocked up the side of the street, and they were comparing notes as to their chances of success. One said to another, "I have a good letter of recommendation from the mayor and one from the supreme judge." Another said, "I have a good letter from Senator So-and-So. I'm sure to get in." The two men came in together and laid their letters down on the commissioners' desk.

"Well," said the officials, "you certainly have many letters, but we won't read them until we measure you." They had forgotten all about that. So the first man is measured, and he is only five feet tall. "No chance for you, sir; the law says the men must be five feet six inches, and you don't come up to the standard."

The other said, "Well, my chances are much better than his. I'm quite a bit taller than he is." He was measuring himself by the other man. That is what people are always doing, measuring themselves by others. Measure yourselves by the law of God or by the Son of God Himself; if you do that, you will find you have come short. He went up to the officers, and they measured him. He was five feet five inches and nine-tenths of an inch. "No good," they told him; "you're not up to the standard."

"But I'm only one-tenth of an inch short," he complained.

"It does not matter," they said; "there's no difference." He left with the man who was five feet tall. One came short six inches and the other only one-tenth of an inch, but the law cannot be changed. And the law of God is that no man will go into the kingdom of heaven with *one* sin on him. He who has broken the least law is guilty of all (James 2:10).

"Is there any hope for me?" you ask. "What star is there to relieve the midnight darkness and gloom? What is to become of me? If all this is true, I am a poor, lost soul. I have committed sin from my earliest childhood." Thank God, my friends, this is where the gospel comes in. *He made Him who knew no sin to be sin for us* (2 Corinthians 5:21). *He was wounded for our transgressions, He was bruised for our iniquities; the chastisement for our peace was upon Him, and by His stripes we are healed. All we like sheep have gone astray; we have turned, every one, to his own way; and the LORD has laid on Him the iniquity of us all* (Isaiah 53:5-6).

You ask me what my hope is; it is that Christ died for my sins, in my place, so I now can enter into life eternal. Paul's hope was the same: *Christ died for our sins according to the Scriptures* (1 Corinthians 15:3). This is the hope in which all the glorious martyrs died, in which all who have entered heaven's gate have found their only comfort. Take that doctrine of substitution out of the Bible, and my hope is gone.

With the law, without Christ, we are all undone. We have broken the law, and it can only hang the sharp sword of justice *What the law could not do for us, He does.* over our head. Even if we could keep it from this moment on, there remains the unforgiven past. *Without shedding of blood there is no remission* (Hebrews 9:22).

Only those who are sheltered behind the finished work of Christ are safe for eternity. What the law could not do for us, He does. He obeyed it to the very letter, and under His obedience we can take our stand. For us He has suffered all its penalties and paid all that the law demands – *who Himself bore our sins in His own body on the tree* (1 Peter 2:24). He saw the awful end from the beginning; He knew what death, what ruin, what misery lay before us if we were left to ourselves. And He came from heaven to teach us the new and living way (Hebrews 10:20); *"by Him everyone who believes is justified from all things from which you could not be justified by the law of Moses"* (Acts 13:39).

There is a well-known story from the time of Napoleon the

First. In one of the war drafts, during one of Napoleon's many wars, a man was drafted who did not want to go, but he had a friend who offered to go in his place. His friend joined the regiment in his name and was sent off to the war. Soon there was a battle in which he was killed, and they buried him on the battlefield. Sometime after, the emperor wanted more men, and by some mistake the first man was drafted a second time. They went to take him, but he protested, "You cannot take me."

"Why not?"

"I am dead," was the reply.

"You are not dead; you are alive and well."

"But I *am* dead," he said.

"You must be mad. Where did you die?"

"At such a battle, and you left me buried on such a battlefield."

"You talk like a madman," they cried, but the man stuck to his story that he had been dead and buried many months. "You look up your books," he said, "and see if it is not so." They looked and found that he was right. They found the man's name entered as drafted, sent to the war, and marked off as killed.

"Look here," they said, "you didn't die; you must have gotten someone to go for you. It must have been your *substitute*."

"I know that," he said. "He died in my place. You cannot touch me: I died in that man, and I go free. The law has no claim against me." They would not recognize the doctrine of substitution, and the case was carried to the emperor. Napoleon said that the man was right, that he was dead and buried in the eyes of the law, and that France had no claim against him.

The story may or may not be true, but one thing I know to be true: the Emperor of heaven recognizes the doctrine of substitution. Christ died for me; that is my hope of eternal life. *There is therefore now no condemnation to those who are in Christ Jesus* (Romans 8:1). If you want to share this blessing, go and deal personally with Christ about it. Take the sinner's place at the foot of the cross. Strip yourself of all your own righteousness and put on Christ's. Wrap yourself in His perfect robe and receive Him by simple trust as your own Savior. That is how you inherit the priceless treasures that Christ has purchased with His blood. *As many as received Him, to them He gave the right to become children of God* (John 1:12). Yes, children of God; He gave the power to overcome the world, the flesh, and the devil; the power to crucify every besetting sin, passion, and lust; and the power to shout in triumph over every trouble and temptation of your life. *I can do all things through Christ who strengthens me* (Philippians 4:13).

I have been trying to tell you the old, old tale that people are sinners. I may be speaking to someone, perhaps, who thinks it is a waste of time. "God knows I'm a sinner," he cries. "You don't need to prove it. Since I could speak, I've done nothing but break every law of earth and heaven." Well, my friend, I have good news for you. It is just as easy for God to save you, even if you have broken every commandment, as the man who has only broken one. Both of you are dead – dead in sins. It does not matter how *dead* you are or how long you have been dead; Christ can bring you to life just the same. There is no difference. When that poor widow came out of Nain, following the body of her darling boy, who had just died, to the grave, Christ's loving heart could not pass her by. He stopped the funeral and commanded the dead to rise. The boy obeyed at once and clasped his mother once more in a living embrace (Luke 7:11-15). And when Jesus stood by the grave of Lazarus, who had been dead *four days,* it was just as easy for Him to say, *"Lazarus, come forth!"* It was just as easy for Him to bring Lazarus, who had been dead four days, from his tomb, as the son of the widow, who had been dead only one. There was no difference. They were both dead, and Christ saved the one just as easily, as willingly, and as lovingly as the other. Therefore, my friend, Christ *can* save you. Christ died *for the ungodly.* And if you turn to Him at this moment with an honest heart and receive Him simply as your Savior and your God, I have the authority of His Word to tell you that He will *by no means cast out* the one who comes to Him (John 6:37).

And you who have never felt the burden of your sin, you who think there is a great deal of difference, you who thank God that you are not as other men – beware. God has nothing to say to the self-righteous. Unless you humble yourself before Him in the dust and confess to Him your iniquities and sins, the gate of heaven, which is open only for *sinners* saved by *grace,* will be shut against you forever.

# GOOD NEWS

*Moreover, brethren, I declare to you the*
*gospel which I preached to you, which also*
*you received and in which you stand.*
– 1 Corinthians 15:1

I do not think there is a word in the English language so little understood as the word *gospel*. We hear it so often, and we have heard it from our earliest childhood, yet there are many people, even many Christians, who do not really know what it means. I believe I was a child of God a long time before I really knew.

The word *gospel* literally means "good news." The gospel is good tidings of great joy. No better news ever came out of heaven than the gospel. No better news ever fell on the ears of the family of man than the gospel. When the angels came down to proclaim the tidings, what did they say to those shepherds on the plains of Bethlehem? "Behold, I bring you *sad* tidings"? No! "Behold, I bring you *bad* news"? No! *"Behold, I bring you good tidings of great joy, which will be to all people. For there is born to you this day in the city of David a Savior"* (Luke 2:10-11).

If those shepherds had been like many people now, they would have said, "We do not believe it is good news. It is all excitement. These angels just want to start a revival. These angels are trying to excite us. Don't believe them." That is what Satan is saying now. "Don't believe the gospel is good news; it will only make you miserable." He knows that the moment a man believes good news, he receives it. And no one who is under the power of the devil really believes that the gospel is good news.

But those shepherds believed the message that the angels brought, and their hearts were filled with joy. If a boy came with a message to someone here, could you not tell by the receiver's looks what kind of a message it was? If it brought good news, you would see it in his face in a moment. If it told him that his boy, a prodigal son away in some foreign land, had come to himself like the one in Luke 15, do you not think that father's face would light up with joy? And if his wife were here, he would not wait until they got home or until she asked for it. He would pass the message over to her, and her face would brighten, too, as she shared his joy.

*We are dead in trespasses and sins, and the gospel offers life.*

But the tidings that the gospel brings are even more glorious than that. We are dead in trespasses and sins, and the gospel offers life. We are enemies to God, and the gospel offers reconciliation. The world is in darkness, and the gospel offers light. Because man will not believe the gospel that Christ is the light of the world, the world is dark today. But the moment a man believes, the light from Calvary crosses his path, and he walks in an unclouded sun.

I want to tell you why I like the gospel. It is because it has been the very best news I have ever heard. That is why I like to preach it, because it has done me so much good. No man can ever tell what it has done for him, but I think I can tell what it has *undone*. It has taken out of my path three of the bitterest enemies I ever had.

There is that terrible enemy mentioned in 1 Corinthians 15, the last enemy, *Death* (1 Corinthians 15:26). The gospel has taken it out of the way. My mind often thinks back to twenty years ago, before I was converted, and how dark the future used to seem. I remember how I used to look on death as a terrible monster who threw his dark shadow across my path, how I trembled as I thought of the terrible hour when he would come for me, and how I wished I would die of some lingering disease, such as tuberculosis, so that I might know when he was coming. It was the custom in our village to toll from the old church bell the age of anyone who died. Every time death entered that village and tore away one of the inhabitants, I counted the tolling of the bell. Sometimes it was seventy, sometimes eighty; sometimes it would be way down among the teens. Sometimes it would toll out the death of someone my own age. It made a solemn impression on me. I felt like a coward then. I thought of the cold hand of death feeling for the cords of life. I thought of being launched to spend my eternity in an unknown land.

As I looked into the grave and saw the sexton throw the earth on the coffin lid, "Earth to earth; ashes to ashes; dust to dust," it seemed like the death knell to my soul. But that is all changed now. The grave has lost its terror. As I go on toward heaven, I can shout, *"O Death, where is your sting?"* (1 Corinthians 15:55), and I hear the answer rolling down from Calvary – "buried in the heart of the Son of God." He took the sting right out of death for me and received it into Himself. If you pluck the stinger out of a hornet, you are not afraid of it after that any more than of a fly. So death has lost its sting. That last enemy has been overcome, and I can look on death as a crushed victim. All that death can get now is this old Adam, and I do not care how quickly I get rid of it. I will get a glorified body, a resurrection body, a body much better than this. If death would come stealing up into this pulpit and lay his icy hand on my heart, causing it to stop beating, I would rise to the better world to be present with the King.

The gospel has made an enemy a friend. What a glorious thought, that when you die, you sink into the arms of Jesus to be carried to the land of everlasting rest! *To die*, the Apostle says, *is gain* (Philippians 1:21). I can imagine when they laid Jesus in Joseph's tomb, one might have seen Death sitting over that grave, saying, "I have Him; He is my victim. He said He was the resurrection and the life. Now I hold Him in my cold embrace. They thought He was never going to die, but look at Him now. He has had to pay tribute to me." Never! The glorious morning comes; the Son of man breaks apart the bands of death and rises, a Conqueror, from the grave. *"Because I live,"* He shouts, *"you will live also"* (John 14:19). Yes, *you will live also* – is it not good news? My friends, there is no bad news about a gospel that makes it so sweet to live and so sweet to die.

Another terrible enemy that troubled me was *Sin*. What a terrible hour I thought it would be, when my sins from childhood, every secret thought, every evil desire, everything done in the dark, would be brought to light and spread out before an assembled universe! Thank God, these thoughts are gone. The gospel tells me my sins are all put away in Christ. Out of love for me, He has taken all my sins and cast them behind His back. That is a safe place for them. God never turns back; He always marches on. He will never see your sins if they are behind His back – that is one of His own illustrations (Luke 4:8). Satan has to get behind God to find them.

How far away are they? Can they ever come back? *As far as the east is from the west, so far has He removed our transgressions from us* (Psalm 103:12). Not some of them; He takes them all away. You may pile up your sins until they rise like a dark mountain and then multiply them by ten thousand for those you cannot think of; and after you have tried to list all the sins you have ever committed, just let me bring one verse in, and that mountain will melt away: *The blood of Jesus Christ His Son cleanses us from all sin* (1 John 1:7).

In Ireland, some time ago, a teacher asked a little boy if there was anything God could not do, and the little guy said, "Yes; He cannot see my sins through the blood of Christ." That is just what He cannot do. The blood covers them. It is good news that you can get rid of sin. You come to Christ a sinner, and if you receive His gospel, your sins are taken away. You are invited to do this; He pleads with you to do it. You are invited to make an exchange: to get rid of all your sins and to receive Christ and His righteousness in the place of them. Is that not good news?

A third enemy that troubled me greatly was *Judgment.* I used to think about the terrible day when I would be summoned before God. I could not tell whether I would hear the voice of Christ saying, *"Depart from Me, you cursed"* (Matthew 25:41) or whether it would be, *"Enter into the joy of your lord"* (Matthew 25:23). And I thought that until he stood before the great white throne, no one could tell whether he was to be on the right hand or the left. But the gospel tells me that is already settled: *There is therefore now no condemnation to those who are in Christ Jesus* (Romans 8:1). *"Most assuredly"* – so we know there is something very important coming – *"Most assuredly, I say to you, he who hears My word and believes in Him who sent Me has everlasting life, and shall not come into judgment, but has passed from death into life"* (John 5:24). I am not coming into judgment for sin. It is not an open question. God's Word has settled it. Christ was judged for me and died in my place, so I go free. He that believes *has.* Is that not good news?

A man prayed for me the other day that I might obtain eternal life at last, in the end. I could not have said amen to that, at least not for the way he said it. You see, I obtained eternal life nineteen years ago when I was converted. What is the gift of God if it is not eternal life? And what makes the gospel such good news? Is it not that it offers eternal life to every poor sinner who will take it? If an angel came straight from the throne of God and proclaimed that God had sent him here to offer us anything we might ask – each one would have his own petition granted – what would be your cry? There would be only one response, and the cry would make heaven ring: "Eternal life! Eternal life!" Everything else would float away into nothingness. It is life we want; it is life we value most. If a man on a sinking ship has millions of dollars and if he could just save his life for six months by giving those millions, he would give them in an instant. But the gospel is not a six months' gift. *The gift of God is eternal life* (Romans 6:23). It is one of the greatest marvels that men have to plead and pray and beg others to take this precious gift of God.

My friends, there is one spot on earth where the fear of Death, Sin, and Judgment can never trouble us, the only safe spot on earth where the sinner can stand – Calvary. In autumn, when men go hunting out in the western country and there has not been any rain for months, sometimes the prairie grass catches fire. When the wind is strong, the flames may be seen rolling along, twenty feet high, destroying man and beast in their onward rush. When the frontiersmen see what is coming, what do they do to escape? They know they cannot run as fast as that fire can run, and the fleetest horse cannot escape it. So they take a match and light the grass around them. The flames sweep onward; they take their stand in the burnt area and are safe. They hear the flames roar as they come along; they see death bearing down on them with overwhelming fury, but they do not fear. They do not even tremble as the ocean of flame surges around them, for over the place where they stand, the fire has already passed, and there is no danger. There is nothing for the fire to burn. And there is one spot on earth that God has swept over. Eighteen hundred years ago the storm burst on Calvary, and the Son of God took it onto Himself, and now, if we take our stand by the cross, we are safe for time and for eternity.

*Oh, receive this gospel tonight – this wonderful message of His sacrifice for you.*

Sinner, do you want to be safe tonight? Do you want to be free from the condemnation of the sins that are past and from the power of the temptations that are to come? Then take your stand on the Rock of Ages. Let death, let the grave, let the judgment come; the victory is Christ's and yours through Him. Oh, receive this gospel tonight – this wonderful message of His sacrifice for you.

Some people, when the gospel is preached, put on a long face, as if they had to attend a funeral or witness an execution or hear some dry, mindless lecture or sermon. It was my privilege to go into Richmond with General Grant's army. I had not been there long before it was announced that the newly freed slaves were going to have a jubilee meeting. These people were just coming into liberty; their chains were falling off, and they were just awakening to the fact that they were free. I thought it would be a great event, and I went down to the African Church, one of the largest in the South, and found it crowded. One of the chaplains of a northern regiment had offered to speak. I have heard many eloquent men in Europe and in America, but I do not think I ever heard eloquence such as I heard that day. He said, "Mothers! Rejoice today. You are forever free! That little child has been torn from your embrace and sold off to some distant state for the last time. Your hearts are never to be broken again in that way; you are free."

The women clapped their hands and shouted at the top of their voices, "Glory, glory to God!" It was good news to them, and they believed it. It filled them full of joy.

Then he turned to the young men, and said, "Young men! Rejoice today. You have heard the crack of the slave driver's whip for the last time. Your posterity will be free. Young men, rejoice today; you are forever free!"

And they clapped their hands and shouted, "Glory to God!" They believed the good tidings.

"Young maidens!" he said. "Rejoice today. You have been put on the auction block and sold for the last time. You are free – forever free!"

They believed it and, lifting up their voices, shouted, "Glory be to God!" I had never been in such a meeting. They *believed* that it was good news to them.

My friends, I bring you better tidings than that. No slave ever had such a mean, wicked, cruel master as those who are serving Satan. Do I speak to a man who is a slave to alcohol? Christ can give you strength to hurl the cup from you and make you a sober man, a loving husband, a kind father. Yes, poor wife, He gives you good news. Your husband may become a sober man again. And you, poor sinner, you who have been so rebellious and wayward, the gospel brings a message of forgiveness to you. God wants you to be reconciled to Him. *Be reconciled to God* (2 Corinthians 5:20). It is His message to you – a message of friendship.

Someone recently told me a little story of reconciliation; perhaps it may help you a little. There was an Englishman who had an only son. Only sons are often spoiled and indulged and ruined. This boy became very headstrong, and, often, he and his father had trouble. One day they had a quarrel, and the father was very angry, and so was the son. The father said he wished the boy would leave home and never come back. The boy said he would go and not come back into his father's house again until he sent for him. The father said he would never send for him. Well, away went the boy. But when a father gives up a boy, a mother does not. You mothers will understand that, but the fathers may not. You know there is no love on earth so strong as a mother's love. A great many things may separate a man and his wife, and a great many things may separate a father from a son; but there is nothing in the whole world that can ever separate a true mother from her child. To be sure, there are some mothers who have drunk so much liquor that they have drunk up all their affection. But I am talking about a true mother, and she would never cast off her boy.

Well, the mother began to write and plead with the boy to write to his father first, and he would forgive him; but the boy said, "I will never go home until father asks me." Then she pled with the father, but the father said, "No, I will never ask him." At last, the mother, brokenhearted, became sick, and when she was told by the physicians that she would die, the husband, anxious to gratify her last wish, wanted to know if there was anything he could do for her before she died. The mother gave him a look; he knew well what it meant.

Then she said, "Yes, there is one thing you can do. You can send for my boy. That is the only wish on earth you can gratify. If you do not pity him and love him when I am dead and gone, who will?"

"Well," said the father, "I will send word to him that you want to see him."

"No," she said, "you know he will not come for me. If I will ever see him, you must send for him." At last, the father went to his office and wrote a dispatch in his own name asking the boy to come home.

As soon as he got the invitation from his father, he started off to see his dying mother. When he opened the door to go in, he found his mother dying and his father by the bedside. The father heard the door open and saw the boy, but instead of going to meet him, he went to another part of the room and refused to speak to him. His mother seized his hand – how she had longed to hold it! She kissed him and then said, "Now, my son, just speak to your father. You speak first, and it will all be over."

But the boy said, "No, mother, I will not speak to him until he speaks to me." She took her husband's hand in one hand and the boy's in the other and spent her final moments trying to bring about a reconciliation. Then just as she was dying – she could not speak – she put the hand of the wayward boy into the hand of the father and passed away! The boy looked at the mother and the father at the wife, and at last, the father's heart broke, and he opened his arms and held that boy; by that body, they were reconciled.

Sinner, that is only a faint type, a poor illustration, because God is not angry with you. I bring you tonight to the dead body of Christ. I ask you to look at the wounds in His hands and feet and the wound in His side. I ask you, "Will you be reconciled?" When He left heaven, He went down into the manger so that He might get a hold of the vilest sinner and put the hand of the wayward prodigal into that of the Father; and He died so that you and I might be reconciled. If you take my advice, you will not sleep tonight until you are reconciled. *Be reconciled to God.* Oh, this gospel of reconciliation! My friends, it is a glad gospel!

*It is a free gospel; anyone may have it.*

And it is a *free* gospel; anyone may have it. You do not need to ask who this good news is for. It is for you. If you would like Christ's own word for it, come with me to that scene in Jerusalem where the disciples are telling Him goodbye. Calvary, with all its horrors, is behind Him; Gethsemane is over, and so is Pilate's judgment hall. He has passed the grave and is about to take His place at the right hand of the Father. Around Him stands His little band of disciples, the little church He was to leave behind Him to be His witnesses. The hour of parting has come, and He has some last words for them. Is He thinking about Himself in these closing moments? Is He thinking about the throne that is waiting for Him and the Father's smile that will welcome Him to heaven? Is He going over in memory the scenes of the past, or is He thinking of the friends who have followed Him so far, who will miss Him so much when He is gone? No, He is thinking about *you*. Did you imagine He would think of those who loved Him? No, sinner, He thought of you then. He thought of His enemies, those who shunned Him, those who despised Him, those who killed Him – He thought what more He could do for them. He thought of those who would hate Him, of those who would have none of His gospel, of those who would say it was too good to be true, of those who would make the excuse that He never died for *them*. Then turning to His disciples, His heart bursting with compassion, He gave them His farewell charge, *"Go into all the world and preach the gospel to every creature"* (Mark 16:15). They are almost His last words, *"to every creature."*

I can imagine Peter saying, "Lord, do you really mean that we should preach the gospel to *every* creature?"

"Yes, Peter."

"Should we go back to Jerusalem and preach the gospel to those Jerusalem sinners who murdered you?"

"Yes, Peter, go back and stay there *until you are endued with power from on high* (Luke 24:49). Offer the gospel to them first. Go look for that man who spat in My face; tell him I will gladly forgive him, if he repents. Go find the man who put that cruel crown of thorns on My brow; tell him I will have a crown ready for him in My kingdom if he will accept salvation. There will not be a thorn in it, and he will wear it forever and ever in the kingdom of his Redeemer. Find that man who took the reed from My hand and struck My head, driving the thorns deeper into My brow. If he will accept salvation as a gift, I will give him a scepter, and he will sway it over the nations of the earth. Yes, I will have him sit with Me on My throne. Go find that man who struck Me with the palm of his hand and preach the gospel to him. Tell him that the blood of Jesus Christ cleanses from all sin (1 John 1:7) and that My blood was shed for him freely, and that all he needs to do is believe." Yes, I can imagine Him saying, "Go, look for that poor soldier who drove the spear into My side. Tell him that there is a nearer way to My heart than that. Tell him that I wish to forgive him freely, and tell him that I will make him a soldier of the cross and that My banner over him will be love" (Song of Solomon 2:4).

I thank God that the gospel is to be preached to *every* creature; I thank God the commission is so free. There is no man so far gone that the grace of God cannot reach him, no man so desperate or so dark that He cannot forgive him. Yes, I thank God I can preach the gospel to the man or the woman who is as dark as hell itself. I thank God for the *whoevers* of the invitations of Christ – *"God so loved the world that He gave His only begotten Son, that whoever believes in Him should not perish but have everlasting life"* (John 3:16) and *Whoever desires, let him take the water of life freely* (Revelation 22:17).

I heard of a woman once who thought there was no promise in the Bible for her; they were all for other people. One day she got a letter and, when she opened it, found it was not for her at all but for some other woman of the same name. It led her to ask herself, "If I find some promise in the Bible directed to *me,* how would I know that it meant *me,* and not some other woman?" She found that she must take God at His word and include herself among the *whoevers* and the *every creatures* to whom the gospel is freely preached. I know that word *whoever* means every man, every woman, every child in this whole world. It means that boy down there, that gray-haired man, that girl in the blush of youth, that young man breaking a mother's heart, that drunk steeped in misery and sin. Oh, my friends, will you not believe this good news? Will you not receive this wonderful gospel of Christ? Will you not believe, poor sinner, that it means *you*? Will you say it is too good to be true?

I was in Ohio a few years ago and was invited to preach in the state prison. Eleven hundred convicts were brought into the chapel, and they all sat in front of me. After I had finished preaching, the chaplain said to me: "Mr. Moody, I want to tell you of a scene that occurred in this room. A few years ago, our commissioners went to the governor of the state and got him to promise that he would pardon five men for good behavior. The governor consented with this understanding – that the record was to be kept secret, and that at the end of six months, the five men highest on the roll would receive a pardon, regardless of who or what they were.

"At the end of six months, the prisoners were all brought into the chapel. The commissioners came up, and the president stood up on the platform. Putting his hand in his pocket, he brought out some papers and said, 'I hold in my hand pardons for five men.'" The chaplain told me he never witnessed anything on earth like it. Every man was as still as death; many were deadly pale. The suspense was awful; it seemed as if every heart had ceased to beat.

The commissioner went on to tell them how they had gotten the pardon, but the chaplain interrupted him. "Before you make your speech, read out the names. This suspense is awful."

So he read out the first name, "Reuben Johnson will come get his pardon." He held it out, but no one came forward. He said to the governor, "Are all the prisoners here?" The governor told him they were all there. Then he said again, "Reuben Johnson will come get his pardon. It is signed and sealed by the governor. He is a free man." No one moved. The chaplain told me he looked right down where Reuben was. He was well known; he had been there nineteen years, and many were looking around to see him spring to his feet. But he himself was looking around to see the fortunate man who had gotten his pardon.

Finally, the chaplain caught his eye and said, "Reuben, you are the man." Reuben turned around and looked behind him to see where Reuben was. The chaplain said the second time, "Reuben, *you* are the man," and a second time he looked around, thinking it must be some other Reuben.

In the same way, men do not believe the gospel is for them. They think it is too good and pass it over their shoulders to the next man. But *you* are the man tonight.

Well, the chaplain could see where Reuben was, and he had to say three times, "Reuben, come get your pardon." At last, the truth began to steal over the old man; he got up and came along down the hall, trembling from head to foot. When he got the pardon, he looked at it, went back to his seat, buried his face in his hands, and wept. When the prisoners got into the ranks to go back to the cells, Reuben got into the ranks, too, and the chaplain had to call to him, "Reuben, get out of the ranks. You are a free man; you are no longer a prisoner." And Reuben stepped out of the ranks. He was free!

That is the way men draw up pardons. They make them out for good character or good behavior, but God fills out pardons for good men *and* for men who do not have any character, who have been very, very bad. He offers a pardon to every sinner if he will take it. I do not care who he is or what he is like. He may be the most immoral man who ever walked the streets, the greatest villain who ever lived, the greatest drunk, thief, or vagabond; but I come tonight with glad news and preach the gospel to *every creature.*

# CHRIST SEEKING SINNERS

*"The Son of Man has come to seek*
*and to save that which was lost."*
– Luke 19:10

To me, this is one of the sweetest verses in the whole Bible. In this one short sentence, we are told what Christ came into this world for. He came for a purpose. He came to do a work, and in this little verse, the whole story is told. He did not come to condemn the world, *but that the world through Him might be saved* (John 3:17).

A few years ago, the Prince of Wales went to America, and there was great excitement about your crown prince coming to our country. The papers reported it and began to discuss it, and many were wondering what he came for. Was it to investigate the republican government? Was it for his health? Was it to see our institutions? Or for this or for that? He came and went, but he never told us what he came for. But when the Prince of Heaven came down into this world, He told us what He came for. God sent Him, and He came to do the will of His Father. What was that? *"To seek and to save that which was lost"* (Luke

19:10). You cannot find any place in Scripture where a man was ever sent by God to do a work in which he failed. God sent Moses to Egypt to bring millions of slaves up out of the house of bondage into the promised land. Did he fail? It looked, at first, as if he were going to. If we had been in the court when Pharaoh said to Moses, *"Who is the* LORD, *that I should obey His voice?"* and ordered him out of his presence (Exodus 5:2), we might have thought it meant failure. But did it? God sent Elijah to stand before Ahab, and it was a bold thing when he told him there would be neither dew nor rain, but he locked up the heavens for three years and six months (1 Kings 17). Now here is God sending His own beloved Son from His bosom, from the throne, down into this world. Do you think He is going to fail? Thanks be to God, He can *save to the uttermost* (Hebrews 7:25), and there is not a person in this city who will not find it so if he is willing to be saved.

I find it a great blessing myself to study a passage like this, looking all around it to see its context and what brought it out. If you look back to the close of Luke 18, you will find Christ coming near the city of Jericho. Sitting by the wayside was a poor, blind beggar. Perhaps he had been there for years, maybe led out by one of his children, or perhaps, as we sometimes see, he had a dog to lead him out. There he had sat for years, and his cry may have been, "Please give a poor, blind man a penny."

One day, as he was sitting there, a man came down from Jerusalem. Seeing the poor blind man, he took his seat by his side and said, "Bartimeus, I have good news for you."

"What is it?" said the blind beggar.

"There is a man in Israel who is able to give you sight."

"Oh, no," said the blind beggar, "there is no chance of me ever receiving sight. I was born blind, and nobody born blind ever got their sight. I will never see in this world. I may in the world to come, but I must go through this world blind."

But the man said, "Let me tell you. I was in Jerusalem the other day, and the great Galilean prophet was there, and I saw a man who was born blind who had received his sight; I never saw a man with better sight. He does not need to use glasses; he can see quite clearly."

Then for the first time, hope rose in the poor man's heart, and he asked, "How was it done?"

"Why, Jesus spat on the ground, made some clay, anointed his eyes, and sent him to wash in the pool of Siloam. While he was doing so, he got two good eyes. It is true. I talked with him, and I didn't see a man in all Jerusalem who had better sight."

"What did He charge?" said Bartimeus.

"Nothing. There was no fee or doctor's bill; he got his sight for nothing. You just tell Him what you want. You don't need to have an influential committee to call on Him or any important delegation. The poor have as much influence with Him as the rich; all are alike."

"What is his name?" asked Bartimeus.

"Jesus of Nazareth. And if He ever comes this way, don't you let Him go by without laying your case before Him."

And the blind man said, "You can be sure of that; He will never pass this way without my seeking Him."

A day or two later, he was led out and took his seat at the usual place, still crying out for money. All at once, he heard the footsteps of a coming multitude and began to ask, "Who is it?" "Tell me, who is it?" Someone said it was Jesus of Nazareth that was passing by. The moment he heard that, he said to himself, "Why, that is the man who gives sight to the blind," and he lifted his voice, *"Jesus, Son of David, have mercy on me!"* (Mark 10:47). Someone, maybe Peter, said to the man, "Hush! Keep still!" He thought the Lord was going up to Jerusalem to be crowned King, and He would not like to be disturbed by a poor, blind beggar. They did not know the Son of God when

He was here! He would hush every harp in heaven to hear a sinner pray; no music delights Him as much.

But Bartimeus lifted his voice louder, *"Son of David, have mercy on me!"* (Mark 10:48). His prayer reached the ear of the Son of God, as prayer always will, and He stopped walking. He told them to bring the man.

"Bartimeus," they said, *"be of good cheer. Rise, He is calling you"* (Mark 10:49). Jesus always had something good for those He called. Oh, sinner! Remember that tonight. They led the blind man to Jesus.

The Lord said, *"What do you want Me to do for you?"*

*"Rabboni, that I may receive my sight."*

*"Go your way; your faith has made you well."* And immediately he received his sight (Mark 10:51-52).

I would have liked to have been there to see that wonderful scene. The first object that met his gaze was the Son of God Himself, and now, among the shouting multitude, no one shouted louder than the poor blind man who had received his sight. He glorified God, and I imagine him shouting "Hosanna to the Son of David" more sweetly than even Mr. Sankey can sing.

Pardon me, if I now draw a little on my imagination. Bartimeus went into Jericho, and he said, "I will go see my wife and tell her about it." A young convert always wants to talk to his friends about salvation. Away he went down the street, and he met a man who passed him, went on a few yards, and then turned back and said, "Bartimeus, is that you?"

"Yes."

"Well, I thought it was, but I could not believe my eyes. How do you have your sight?"

"Oh, I just met Jesus of Nazareth outside the city and asked Him to have mercy on me."

"Jesus of Nazareth! Is He in this part of the country?"

"Yes. He is right here in Jericho. He is now going down to the western gate."

"I would like to see Him," said the man, and he ran down the street, but because he was short and there was a great crowd around Jesus, the man could not catch a glimpse of Him, even though he stood on tiptoe.

"Well," he said, "I am not going to be disappointed," so he ran on and climbed up into a sycamore tree. "If I can get on to that branch hanging right over the highway, He cannot pass by without my getting a good look at Him." It must have been a very strange sight to see the rich man climbing up a tree like a boy and hiding among the leaves where he thought nobody would see him to get a glimpse of the passing stranger!

The crowd burst out, and he looked for Jesus. He looked at Peter; "That is not He." He looked at John; "That is not He." At last, his eye rested on One fairer than the sons of men; "That is He!" And Zaccheus, just peeping out from among the branches, looked down on the wonderful God-man in amazement. At last, the crowd came to the tree. Perhaps Zaccheus thought that Christ would pass on without seeing him, but the Lord stopped right under the tree, looked up, and said, *"Zaccheus, make haste and come down"* (Luke 19:5). I can imagine the first thought in his mind

> You do not need to try to hide from Him.

was, "Who told Him my name? I was never introduced to Him." Ah! Christ knew him. Sinner, Christ knows all about you. He knows your name and where you live. You do not need to try to hide from Him. He knows where you are and all about you.

Some people do not believe in sudden conversion. I would like them to answer me: When was Zaccheus converted? He was certainly in his sins when he went up into that tree; he certainly was converted when he came down. He must have been converted somewhere between the branch and the ground. It didn't take a long time to convert that publican! *"Make haste and come down. I will never pass this way again; this is my last* visit." Zaccheus made haste, came down, and received Him joyfully. Did you ever hear of any one receiving Christ in any other way? He received Him joyfully. Christ brings joy with Him. Sin, gloom, and darkness flee away; light, peace, and joy burst into the soul. May there be many that come down from their high places and receive Christ tonight!

Someone may ask, "How do you know that he was converted?" I think he gave very good evidence. I would like to see as fruitful evidence of conversion here tonight. Let some of you rich men be converted and give half your goods to feed the poor, and people will believe pretty quickly that it is genuine work! But there is even better evidence than that. *"If I have taken anything from anyone by false accusation, I restore fourfold"* (Luke 19:8). That is very good evidence. You say if people are converted suddenly, they won't hold out, they won't persevere. Zaccheus held out long enough to restore fourfold. We would like to have a work of the Spirit that reaches men's pockets.

I can imagine one of Zaccheus's servants going to a neighbor the next morning and handing over to him thousands of dollars.

"What is this for?" the neighbor asks.

"Oh, my master defrauded you of a few hundred dollars several years ago, and this is restitution money." That would give confidence in Zaccheus's conversion! I wish a few cases like that would happen here, and then people would stop talking against sudden conversions.

The Lord goes to be the publican's guest, and while He is there, the Pharisees begin to murmur and complain. It would have been a good thing if Pharisees had died off with that generation, but, unfortunately, they have left a good many grandchildren living down here now who are always complaining, *"This Man receives sinners"* (Luke 15:2). But while the Pharisees were complaining, the Lord uttered the words I have read tonight; it is as if He had said, "I did not come to Zaccheus to make him wretched, to condemn him, to torment him; I came to bless and save him. *"The Son of Man has come to seek and to save that which was lost."*

If there is a man or woman in this audience tonight who believes that he or she is *lost,* I have good news – Christ has come seeking you. I was at the Fulton Street prayer meeting one Saturday night many years ago, and when the meeting was over, a man came to me and said, "I would like to have you go down to the city prison tomorrow and preach to the prisoners. I said I would be very glad to go. There was no chapel in connection with that prison, and I was to preach to them in their cells. I had to stand at a little iron railing and talk down a great, long narrow passageway to some three or four hundred of them, I suppose, all out of sight. It was pretty difficult work; I had never preached to bare walls before. When it was over, I thought I would like to see to whom I had been preaching and how they had received the gospel. I went to the first door, where the inmates could have heard me best, and looked in at a little window, and there were some men playing cards. I suppose they had been playing all the while.

"How are you doing here?" I asked.

"Well, stranger, we don't want you to get a bad idea of us. False witnesses lied, and that is how we are here."

"Oh," I said, "Christ cannot save anybody here; there is nobody *lost.*" I went to the next cell. "Well, friend, how is it with you?"

"Oh," said the prisoner, "the man that did the deed looked very much like me, so they caught me, and I am here." He was innocent too! I passed along to the next cell. "How is it with you?"

"Well, we got into bad company, and the man that did it got away, and we got caught, but we never did anything."

I went along to the next cell. "How is it with you?"

"Our trial is next week, but they have nothing against us, and we'll get free."

I went around to nearly every cell, but the answer was always the same – they had never done anything. Why, I never saw so many innocent men together in my life! There was nobody to blame but the judges, according to their way of thinking. These men were wrapping their filthy rags of self-righteousness around them. And that has been the story for thousands of years. I got discouraged as I went through the prison, cell after cell, and every man had an excuse. If he didn't already have one, the devil helped him to make one. I was almost all the way through the prison when I came to a cell and found a man with his elbows on his knees, and his head in his hands. Two little streams of tears were running down his cheeks; they were no longer coming by drops.

"What's the trouble?" I asked. He looked up, the picture of remorse and despair.

"Oh, my sins are more than I can bear."

"Thank God for that," I replied.

"What? You are the man that has been preaching to us, ain't you?"

"Yes."

"I think you said you were a *friend?*"

"I am."

"And yet you are glad that my sins are more than I can bear!"

"I will explain," I said. "If your sins are more than you can bear, won't you cast them on One who will bear them for you?"

"Who is that?"

"The Lord Jesus."

"He won't bear *my* sins."

"Why not?"

"I have sinned against Him all my life."

"I don't care if you have. The blood of Jesus Christ, God's Son, cleanses from all sin." Then I told him how Christ had come to seek and save that which was lost and to open the prison doors

56

and set the captives free. It was like a cup of cold water to find a man who believed he was lost, so I stood there and told him about a crucified Savior. "Christ was delivered for our offenses, died for our sins, rose again for our justification" (Romans 4:25). For a long time, the man could not believe that such a miserable wretch could be saved. He went on to list his sins, and I told him that the blood of Christ could cover them all. After I had talked with him, I said, "Now let us pray." He got down on his knees inside the cell, and I got down outside, and I said, "You pray."

"Why," he said, "it would be blasphemy for me to call on God."

"You call on God," I said. He knelt down, and, like the poor publican, he lifted up his voice and said, "God be merciful to me, a vile wretch!" I put my hand through the window, and as I shook hands with him, a tear fell on my hand that burned down into my soul. It was a tear of repentance. He believed he was lost. Then I tried to get him to believe that Christ had come to save him. I left him still in darkness. "I will be at the hotel," I said, "between nine and ten o'clock, and I will pray for you."

The next morning, I was so interested in him that I thought I must see him before I went back to Chicago. As soon as I saw his face, I knew that remorse and despair had fled away. His countenance was beaming with celestial light; the tears of joy had come into his eyes, and the tears of despair were gone. The Sun of Righteousness had shone out across his path. His soul was leaping within him for joy; he had received Christ as Zaccheus did – joyfully.

"Tell me about it," I said.

"Well, I do not know what time it was; I think it was about midnight. I had been in distress a long time, when all at once my great burden fell off, and now I believe I am the happiest man in New York."

I think he was the happiest man I saw from the time I left Chicago until I got back again. His face was lit up with the light that comes from the celestial hills. I told him goodbye, and I expect to meet him in another world.

Can you tell me why the Son of God came down to that prison that night, and, passing cell after cell, went to that one and set the captive free? It was because the man believed he was lost.

But you say, *"I do not feel that."* Well, never mind your feelings; *believe* it. Just ask yourself, "Am I saved, or am I lost?" It must be one or the other. There is no neutrality about the matter. A man cannot be saved and lost at the same time; it is impossible. If the Bible is true, every man and woman in this audience must either be saved or lost. If I did not think it was true, I would not be here preaching, and I would not advise you people to come; but if the Bible is true, every man and every woman in this room must either be in the ark or out of it, either *saved* or *lost*.

I do not believe there would be a dry eye in this city tonight if men would wake up to the thought of what it is to be lost. The world has been rocked to sleep by Satan, who is going up and down telling people that it doesn't mean anything. I believe in the biblical heaven and hell. Christ came down to save us from a terrible hell, and any man who is cast down to hell must go in the full blaze of the gospel and over the mangled body of the Son of God.

When we hear of a man who has lost his health, we sympathize with him, and we say it is very sad. Our hearts are drawn out in sympathy. When another has lost his wealth, we say, "That is very sad." And when a man loses his reputation, his standing among men, "That is sadder still," you say. We know what it is to lose health and wealth and reputation, but what is the loss of all these things compared with the loss of the soul?

I was in an eye hospital in Chicago some time ago, before the great fire. A mother brought a beautiful little baby to the doctor – a baby only a few months old – and wanted the doctor to look at the child's eyes. He did so and pronounced it blind – blind for life – it will never see again. The moment he said that, the mother seized the baby, pressed it to her chest, and gave a terrible scream. It pierced my heart, and I could not help weeping. What a fearful thought to that mother! "Oh, my darling" she cried, "are you never to see the mother who gave you birth? Oh, doctor, I cannot stand it. My child, my child!" It was a sight to move any heart. But what is the loss of eyesight to the loss of a soul? I would much rather have these eyes taken out of my head and go to the grave blind than lose my soul. I have a son, and only God knows how I love him; but I would see those eyes dug out of his head tonight rather than see him grow up to manhood and go down to the grave without Christ and without hope. The loss of a soul! Christ knew what it meant. That is what brought Him from the bosom of the Father; that is what brought Him from the throne. That is what brought Him to Calvary. The Son of God was resolute. When He died on Calvary, it was to save a lost world; it was to save your soul and mine.

*Oh, the loss of the soul – how terrible it is!*

Oh, the loss of the soul – how terrible it is! If tonight you feel that you are lost, I beg you to not rest until you have found peace in Christ. Fathers and mothers, if you have children out of the ark, do not rest until they are brought into it. Do not discourage your children from coming to Christ. I am glad to see those little boys and girls here. Dear children, remember the sermon is for *you*. The Son of Man came for you as much as for that old gray-haired man over there. He came for all, rich and poor, young and old. Young man, if you are lost, may God show it to you, and may you run into the kingdom. The Son of Man has come to seek and to save you.

There is a story told of Rowland Hill.[2] He was once preach-

---

2   Rowland Hill (1745-1833) was a popular English pastor. He also established schools for poor girls, Sunday schools, and a clinic to vaccinate thousands of children.

ing in the open air to a large audience. Lady Anne Erskine was riding by, and she asked who it was that was addressing the vast assembly. When she was told it was the celebrated Rowland Hill, she said, "I have heard of him; drive me near the platform so that I may listen to him." The eye of Rowland Hill rested on her; he saw that she belonged to the nobility, and turning to someone, he inquired who she was. He went on preaching, and then all at once, he stopped.

"My friends," he said, "I have got something here for sale." Everybody was startled to think that a minister was going to sell something in his sermon. "I am going to sell it by auction, and it is worth more than the crown of all Europe: it is the soul of Lady Anne Erskine. Will anyone bid for her soul? I think I hear a bid. Who bids? Satan bids. What will you give?"

"I will give riches, honor, and pleasure; yes, I will give the whole world for her soul," Satan answered.

"Listen! I hear another bid for this soul. Who bids? The Lord Jesus Christ. Jesus, what will you give for this soul?"

"I will give peace, joy, and comfort that the world does not know. I will give eternal life for her soul."

Turning to Lady Anne Erskine, he said, "You have heard the two bidders for your soul – who will have it?"

She ordered the footman to open the door, and pushing her way through the crowd, she said, "The Lord Jesus will have my soul if He will accept it." That may be true, or it may not, but there is one thing I *know* to be true – there are two bidders for your soul tonight. It is for you to decide who will have it. Satan offers you what he cannot give; he is a liar and has been from the foundation of the world. I pity the man who is living on the devil's promises. He lied to Adam, deceived him, stripped him of all he had, and then left him in his lost, ruined condition. And all men since Adam, living on the devil's lies, the devil's promises, have been disappointed and will be, down to the end of time. But the Lord Jesus Christ is able to give all He offers, and He offers eternal life to every lost soul here. *The gift of God is eternal life* (Romans 6:23). Who will take it? Will anyone shout here tonight that you want to be saved and let it go up to the throne of God? As Mr. Sankey sang of that shout around the throne, my heart went up to God that there might be a great shout for lost ones brought home tonight.

Last night a man told me he was anxious to be saved, but Christ had never sought him. I said, "What are you waiting for?"

"Why," he said, "I am waiting for Christ to call me; as soon as He calls me, I am coming." There may be others here who have got the same notion. Now, I do not believe there is a person in this city that the Spirit of God has not worked on at some period of his life. I do not believe there is a person in this audience that Christ has not sought after. Bear in mind, He takes the place of the seeker. Every man who has ever been saved was first sought after by God. No sooner did Adam fall than God sought him. He had gone away frightened and hid himself among the bushes in the garden, but God took the place of the seeker. From that day to this, God has always had the place of the seeker. No man or woman in this audience has been saved that God did not seek first.

What do we read in Luke 15? There is a shepherd bringing home his sheep into the fold. As they pass in, he stands and numbers them. I can see him counting one, two, three, up to ninety-nine. "But," he said, "I ought to have one hundred; I must have made a mistake," and he counts them over again. "There are only ninety-nine here; I must have lost one." He does not say, "I will let him find his own way back." No! He takes the place of the seeker; he goes out into the mountain and hunts until he finds the lost one, and then he lays it on his shoulder and brings it home. Is it the sheep that finds the shepherd? No, it is the shepherd who finds and brings back the sheep. He rejoiced to find it. Undoubtedly, the sheep was very glad to get back to the fold, but it was the shepherd who rejoiced and who called his friends and said, *"Rejoice with me"* (Luke 15:6).

Then there is that woman who lost the piece of money. Someone perhaps had paid her a bill that day, giving her ten pieces of silver. As she retires at night, she takes the money out of her pocket and counts it. "Why," she says, "I have only nine pieces; I ought to have ten." She counts it over again. "Only nine pieces! Where have I been," she says, "since I got that money? I am sure I have not been out of the house." She turns her pocket wrong side out, and there she finds a hole in it. Does she wait until the money gets back into her pocket? No. She takes a broom and lights a candle and sweeps diligently. She moves the sofa and the table and the chairs and all the rest of the furniture and sweeps in every corner until she finds it. And when she has found it, who rejoices? The piece of money? No; the woman who finds it. In these parables, Christ brings out the great truth that God takes the place of seeker. People talk of finding Christ, but it is Christ who first finds them.

Another young man told me last night that he was too great a sinner to be saved, but they are the very men Christ came after. *"This Man receives sinners and eats with them"* (Luke 15:2). The only charge they could bring against Christ down here was that He was receiving bad men. They are the very kind of men He is willing to receive. All you have to do is to prove that you are a sinner, and I will prove that you have a Savior. And the greater the sinner, the greater need you have of a Savior. You say your heart is hard; then, of course, you want Christ to soften it. You cannot do it yourself. The harder your heart, the more need you have of Christ; the blacker your sin, the more need you have of a Savior. If your sins rise up before you like a dark mountain, bear in mind that the blood of Jesus Christ cleanses from all sin. There is no sin so big, so dark, or so corrupt and vile that the blood of Christ cannot cover it. So I preach the old gospel again, *"The Son of Man has come to seek and to save that which was lost."*

It was Adam's fall, his *loss,* that brought out God's love. God never told Adam when He put him into Eden that He loved him. It was his fall, his sin, that brought it out. A friend of mine from Manchester was in Chicago a few years ago, and he was very interested in the city – a great city, with its 300,000 or 400,000 inhabitants, with its great railway centers, its lumber market, its pork market, and its grain market. He said he went back to Manchester and told his friends about Chicago. But he could not get anybody very interested in it. It was very far away, and the people did not seem to want to hear about it.

*The blacker your sin, the more need you have of a Savior.*

But one day there came on the news the sad tidings that it was on fire, and, my friend said, the Manchester people became suddenly interested in Chicago! They read every message, bought all the papers, and devoured every particle of news. And at last, when the news came that Chicago was burning up, that 100,000 people were turned out of house and home, then everyone became so interested that they began to weep for us. They came forward and laid down their money – some gave thousands of dollars – for the relief of the poor sufferers. It was the *calamity* of Chicago that brought out the love of Manchester and of London and of Liverpool. I was in that terrible fire, and I saw men who were wealthy stripped of all they had. When they had gone to bed that Sunday night, they were the richest men in Chicago. The next morning, they were paupers, but I did not see a man weep. But when the news came, "Liverpool is giving thousands of dollars; Manchester is giving thousands of dollars; London is giving money to aid the city;" and as the news kept flashing that help was coming, Chicago was brokenhearted. I saw men weep then. The love that was shown to us, that love broke our hearts. So the love of God ought to break every heart in this city. It was love that brought Christ down here to die for us. It was love that made Him leave His place by the Father's throne and come down here *to seek and to save that which was lost.*

But now for the sake of these who believe Christ never sought them, perhaps it would be good to say *how* He seeks. There are many ways He does. Last night I found a man looking for help, and the Lord had been speaking to him by the prayers of a godly sister who died a little while ago. Her prayers were answered. He came trembling from head to foot. I talked to him about the plan of salvation; the tears trickled down his cheeks, and at last he trusted Christ as his Savior. The Son of Man sought out that young man through the prayers of his sister and then through her death.

Some of you had godly, praying mothers who have prayed whole nights for your soul and who have now gone to heaven. Did you not take their hand and promise that you would meet them there? That was the Son of God seeking you by your mother's prayers and your mother's death. Some of you have faithful, godly ministers who weep for you in the pulpit and plead with you to come to Christ. You have heard heart-searching sermons; the truth has gone down deep into your heart, and tears have run down your cheeks. That was the Son of God seeking you.

Some of you have had godly, praying Sunday school teachers who urged you to come to Christ. Some of you, perhaps, have Christian young men around you, and they have talked with you and pleaded with you to come to Christ. That was the Son of God seeking after your soul. Some of you have had a tract put in your hand with a startling title, "Eternity; Where Will You Spend It?" and the arrow has hit home. That was the Son of God seeking after you. Many of you have been ill and you have had time to think and meditate. In the silent watches of the night, when everybody was asleep, the Spirit of God has come into your room, has come to your bedside, and the thought came stealing through your mind that you ought to be a child of God and an heir of heaven. That was the Son of God seeking after your lost soul. Some of you have had little children, and you have laid them in the cemetery. When that little child was dying, you promised to love and serve God (Have you kept your promise?). That was the Son of God seeking you. He took that little child to draw your affections toward heaven.

It would take me all night to tell the different ways in which the Lord seeks. Can you stand in this hall tonight and say that the Son of God never sought for you? I do not believe there is a man or woman in this audience or in the whole city who could do it. My friend, He has been calling for you from your earliest childhood, and He has put it into the hearts of God's own people to call you together in this hall. Prayer is going up all over the Christian world for you. Perhaps there never has been a time in the history of your life when so many were praying for you as at the present time. That is the Son of God seeking for your soul through the prayers of the church, through the prayers of ministers, through the prayers of the saints not only here in London but throughout the world. I have received news today in a message sent from America that nearly all the churches in America are praying for London. What does it mean? God has laid it on the heart of the church throughout the world to pray for London. It must be that God has something good in store for London. The Son of Man is coming to London to seek and to save that which was lost, and I pray that the Good Shepherd may enter this hall tonight and may come to many hearts. May you hear the still small voice: *"Behold, I stand at the door and knock. If anyone hears My voice and opens the door, I will come in to him and dine with him, and he with Me"* (Revelation 3:20). O friends, open the door tonight and let the heavenly Visitor in. Do not turn Him away any longer. Do not say with Felix, *"Go away for now; when I have a convenient time I will call for you"* (Acts 24:25). Make this a convenient time; make this the night of your salvation. Receive the gift of God tonight. Open the door of your heart, and say, "Welcome, thrice welcome, into this heart of mine."

# SINNERS SEEKING CHRIST

*Seek the LORD while He may be found,*
*call upon Him while He is near.*
– Isaiah 55:6

I have been speaking about the Son of Man seeking the lost; now I want to look at the other side – man's side. I have learned that when anyone becomes serious about his soul's salvation, he begins to seek God, and it does not take a long time for them to meet. It does not take long for an anxious sinner to meet an anxious Savior. *You will seek Me and find Me, when you search for Me with all your heart* (Jeremiah 29:13). These are the people who find Christ – those who seek for Him with all their heart. I am tired and sick of halfheartedness. You don't like a halfhearted man; you don't care for anyone to love you with half a heart, and the Lord does not want it either. If we are going to seek Him and find Him, we must do it with all our heart.

I believe the reason why so few people find Christ is because they do not search for Him with all their heart; they are not *terribly* serious about their souls' salvation. *God* is in earnest;

everything God has done proves that He is zealous about the salvation of men's souls. He has proved it by giving His only Son to die for us. The Son of God was in earnest when He died. Calvary is proof of that. And the Lord wants us to be serious when it comes to this great question of the soul's salvation. People seeking Him with all their hearts soon find Him.

It was quite refreshing last night to find a young man who thought he was not worth saving because he was so vile and wicked. There was hope for him because he was so desperately serious about his soul. He thought he was worthless. He saw himself in God's mirror, and when a man does that, he has a very poor opinion of himself. You can always tell when a man is far from God – he is always talking about himself and how good he is. But the moment he sees God with the eye of faith, he is down on his knees, and, like Job, he cries, *"Behold, I am vile"* (Job 40:4). All his goodness flees away. What people need is to be in earnest about their salvation, and they will soon find Christ. You do not need to go up to the heights to bring Him down or down to the depths to bring Him up or to go off to some distant city to find Him. This day He is near to every one of us. I heard someone telling a young person to go home and seek Christ in his room. I would not dare to tell anyone to do that. You might be dead before you got home. If I read my Bible correctly, the man who preaches the gospel is not the man who tells me to seek Christ tomorrow or an hour from now, but *now*. He is near to every one of us this minute to save. If the world would just come to God for salvation and be sincere about it, they would find the Son of God right at the door of their heart.

Suppose I should say I lost a very valuable diamond here last night – I have not, but just imagine I had – worth millions of dollars. I had it in my pocket when I came into the hall, and when I had finished preaching, I found it was not in my pocket but must be in the hall somewhere. And suppose I was to say that anyone who found it could have it. How serious you would all become! You would not get very much out of my sermon; you would all be thinking of the diamond. I do not believe even the police could get you out of this hall. The idea of finding a diamond worth millions of dollars! If you could only find it, it would lift you out of poverty at once, and you would be independent for the rest of your days. Oh, how soon everybody would be zealous then! I would love to get men to seek for Christ in the same way. I have something worth more than a diamond to offer you. Is not salvation – eternal life – worth more than all the diamonds in the world?

*There is nothing that men value as they do life.*

Suppose Gabriel would wing his way from the throne of God and come down here and say he had been commissioned by Jehovah to come and offer to this assembly any one gift you might choose. You could have just what you chose but only one thing. What would it be? The wealth of England or of the world? Would that be your choice? Ten thousand times, no! Your one cry would be, "Life! Eternal life!"

There is nothing that men value as they do life. If a man worth millions of dollars is out on a sinking ship and his only chance is to give up those millions just to save the life of the body, he would give it up in a moment. *"Skin for skin! Yes, all that a man has he will give for his life"* (Job 2:4). I understand some people have been afraid to come to this hall because there might be a cry of "Fire! Fire!" and in a panic, they might lose their lives. Yet there are twenty doors to the building; I do not know that I ever saw a building that you could more easily get out of. Yet people seem to sleep and forget that there is no door out of hell. If they enter there, they must remain age after age. Millions and millions of years will roll on, but there will be no door, no escape out of hell. May God wake up this slumbering congregation and make you anxious about your souls.

People talk about our being earnest and fanatical – about our being on fire. I wish the church was on fire; this world would soon shake to its foundation. May God wake up a slumbering church! We do not want people to shout "Amen" or clasp their hands. The deepest and quietest waters very often run swiftest. We want you to go right to work; there will be a chance for you to shout later. Go speak to your neighbor and tell him of Christ and heaven. You need only to go a few yards down these streets before you find someone who is passing down to the darkness of eternal death. Let us hurry to the rescue!

We want to see people really wishing to become Christians, people who are dead serious about it. If someone were to ask you if you want to become a Christian and you reply, "Well, *I would not mind,*" my friend, until you change your language, I do not think *you* will ever get into the kingdom of God. We want people crying from the depths of their heart, "I *want* to be saved." On the day of Pentecost, the cry was, *"Men and brethren, what shall we do?"* (Acts 2:37). These men were in earnest, and they found Christ right there; three thousand found Him when they sought Him with all their hearts.

When men seek Christ as they do wealth, they will soon find Him. To be sure, the world will raise a cry that they are excited. Let stock go up ten or fifteen percent before tomorrow morning, and you will see how quickly people will get excited! And the news doesn't play it down either. They say it is healthy excitement; commerce is prospering. But when you begin to get excited about your soul's salvation and are serious about it, then they raise the cry, "Oh, they are getting excited. That isn't healthy." Yet they don't talk about men rushing down to death by the thousands. There is a poor drunk, look at him! Hear the piercing cry going up to heaven! Yet the church of God slumbers and sleeps. Sometimes, a few will ask some questions, but they go about it as if they were half asleep. When will people seek Christ as they seek wealth or honor?

I am told that when the war broke out on the Gold Coast, though it was known that the climate was a very unhealthy one and many who went there would never return, thousands of men wanted to go. Why? They wanted to get wealth and from wealth, honor. And if there is a chance of going to India, men are always willing to go. To get a little honor, they will sacrifice comfort, pleasure, health, and everything. What we want is to have people seeking the kingdom of God as they seek celebrity, honor, and wealth.

As I said, if life is in danger, how terribly serious men become. There is no doubt about *that*. But why should people not be as serious about their soul's salvation? Why should every man and woman here not wake up and seek the Lord with all their heart? It is then, the Lord says, that you *will* find Him.

There is a story told of a ship that was going down at sea. There were not enough lifeboats to take all on board. When the vessel went down, some of the lifeboats were near the ship. A man swam to one of the lifeboats from the wreck just as it was going down, but they had no room to take him, and they refused. When they refused, he grabbed hold of the boat with his right hand, but they took a sword and cut off his fingers. When he had lost the fingers of his right hand, the man was so determined to save his life that he seized the boat with his left hand; they cut off the fingers of that hand too. Then the man swam up and seized the boat with his teeth, and they had compassion on him and relented. They could not cut off his head, so they took him in, and the man saved his life. Why? *Because he was in earnest.* Why not seek your soul's salvation as that man sought to save his life?

Will there ever be a better time? Will there ever be a better time for that old man whose hair is growing gray, whose eyes are growing dim, and who is hastening to the grave? Is this not the very best time for him? *Seek the LORD while He may he found* (Isaiah 55:6). There is a man in the middle of life. Is this not the best time for him to seek the kingdom of God? Will you ever have a better opportunity? Will Christ ever be more willing to save than now? He says, *"Come, for all things are now ready"* (Luke 14:17). Not *going to be ready* but are *now* ready. Young man, my friend, is now not the best time for you to seek the kingdom of God? Seek the Lord; you can find Him here tonight. Can you say that you will find Him here tomorrow? Will anyone stand up in this hall and say that? Young man, you do not know what tomorrow will bring. Do you know that since we met here last night, forty-three thousand souls have passed from time to eternity? Do you know that every time the clock ticks, a soul passes away? Is this not the best time for you to seek the kingdom of God? My boy, the Lord wants you. *Seek first the kingdom of God* (Matthew 6:33), and seek Him while He may be found.

> My friend, is now not the best time for you to seek the kingdom of God?

In the 1850s, a great revival swept over America. Many men stood and shook their heads; they could not believe it was a healthy state of things. The church was not in its normal state! The church from Maine to Minnesota and on to California was astir. And as you passed over the great republic, over its western prairies and mountains, through its valleys, through its cities and villages, you could see the churches lit up, and people were flocking into the kingdom of God by the hundreds. And in a year and a half or two years, there were more than half a million souls brought in. People said it was false excitement, wildfire, and it would pass away. But, my friends, it was grace preceding judgment. Little did we know that our nation was soon to be baptized in blood and that we would soon hear the tramp of a million men, that thousands of our young men, the flower of our nation, would soon be lying in a soldier's grave.

My friends, it was God calling His people in. He was preparing our nation for a terrible struggle.

And now, it seems to me that there is another wave of blessing passing over this earth. News is coming from all parts of the world, telling us of the great work God is doing. The last news from India told us of a blessed work going on there. The news from Japan and from other places tell the same good news of God pouring out His Spirit. Just the other day, two men came up here from a town of fifty thousand inhabitants and wanted us to go there, but we could not. We told them to go home and get to work themselves. Today one of them told us that they had sixteen last night asking about salvation. God is pouring out His Spirit everywhere. Everywhere men are putting in the sickle, *for the harvest is ripe* and bringing their sheaves and laying them at the feet of the Master (Joel 3:13). I believe we are living in the days that our fathers prayed for. The heavens are opened, and the Spirit of God is descending on the sons of men.

This time of revival is a good time to seek the Lord. Will you ever have a better time? The news from every city is this – the people are praying. I have wondered if there was ever so much prayer going up to God as at the present. Not only here, but all around the world, we have God's people with their hearts burdened for the salvation of souls. Is God not working? Will there ever be a better time for you to seek the kingdom of God than now, when there is such a great awakening, when there is such a spirit of expectation, when the church of God is coming as one, and when the spirit of unity prevails? Think of the ones praying here. Do you believe there were ever so many men and women praying for your soul as there are here tonight? Look over this audience – what are these Christians doing now? They are silently praying to God. I can see they are praying. There is a young man with his mother sitting by his side. That mother is pleading, "God, save my boy tonight!" May it go down deep into his soul! *Seek the Lord while He may be found.*

Let me ask you a question. Do you believe that the Lord can be found here tonight? I ask these ministers present at my side; do you believe He can? They answer yes. My friends, do *you* believe it? Another yes comes from the audience. Well, if He can, is it not the height of madness for any man or woman to go out of this hall without seeking Him? If He can be found, why not seek Him? Young lady, why not seek Him with all your heart? Young man, why not seek Christ tonight with all your heart? Why not say, "I *must* be saved"? There is nothing so important as this great question of salvation.

If you could win the world, what would you do with it? Would it be worth as much as Christ? Lay everything else aside and make up your minds that you will not rest until you have sought and found the Lord Jesus. Everyone I ever knew who made up his mind to seek Him soon found Him. In Dublin a young man found Christ. He went home and lived a life so godly and so Christlike that two of his brothers could not understand what had brought the change in him. They left Dublin, followed us to Sheffield, and found Christ there. They were in earnest.

But thank God you do not have to go out of this hall. Christ can be found here tonight. I firmly believe every one of you can find Christ tonight if you will seek Him with all your heart. He says, "Call on Me." Did you ever hear of anyone wholeheartedly calling on Christ that Christ did not answer? Look at that thief on the cross! Perhaps he had a praying mother, and she taught him Isaiah 55. He had heard Christ pray that wonderful prayer, *"Father, forgive them"* (Luke 23:34). And as he was hanging on the cross, that text of Scripture came to his mind, *Seek the* LORD *while He may be found, call upon Him while He is near* (Isaiah 55:6). The truth came flashing into his soul, and he said, "He is near me now; I will call on Him. *Lord, remember me when You come into Your kingdom"* (Luke 23:42). No sooner had he called than the Lord said, *"Today you will be with Me in*

*Paradise"* (Luke 23:43). That was his seeking opportunity, his day. My friends, this is your day now. I believe that every man has his day. You have it just now; why not call on Him just now?

Say as the poor thief did, *"Lord, remember me!"* That was his golden opportunity, and the Lord heard, answered, and saved him. Bartimeus called on Him while He was near. Christ was passing from Jericho for the last time, and Bartimeus cried out, *"Son of David, have mercy on me!"* (Luke 18:39). The Lord heard his prayer and gave him his sight. It was a good thing that Zaccheus called – or rather that the Lord called him; but when the Lord called, he came. May the Lord call many here, and may you respond, "Lord, here am I. You have called, and I come." Do you believe the Lord will call a poor sinner and then cast him out? No! His word stands forever: *"The one who comes to Me I will by no means cast out"* (John 6:37).

I was glad when that man I told you of said he felt as if he was too bad. Men are pretty near the kingdom of God when they do not see anything good in themselves. At the Fulton Street prayer meeting, a man came in, and this was his story. He said he had a mother who prayed for him; he was a wild, reckless prodigal. Sometime after his mother's death, he began to be troubled. He thought he ought to make new friends and leave his old companions. So he said he would go join a secret society; he thought he would join the Odd Fellows. They inquired about him before admitting him to membership, and when they found out he was a drunken sailor, they blackballed him. They would not have him. He then went to the Freemasons. He had nobody to recommend him, so they inquired and found there was no good in his character, and they too blackballed him. They didn't want him. One day, someone handed him a little notice in the street about the prayer meeting, and he went in. He heard that Christ had come to save sinners. He believed Him. He took Him at His word, and in reporting the matter, he said he "came to Christ without character, and Christ hadn't blackballed him."

My friends, that is Christ's way. Is there a man here without character, without references, with nobody to say a good word for him? I bring you good news. Call on the Son of God, and He will hear you. Call on Him tonight.

I was at a meeting for ministers the other day. Up in the balcony, there was one solitary woman; she sat there alone. When the meeting was over and I was leaving, she came and said, "Mr. Moody, do you remember me?"

"Oh, yes," I said, "I remember you." Where had I met her? Mr. Sankey and I were leaving Dundee for the north of Scotland. There was a lady who had come from London and brought her two boys all the way to get blessed. They must have been about eighteen or nineteen – twins. That mother's heart was burdened for their salvation. The last night we had a meeting there, one of the sons yielded himself to Christ, and the mother went back the next morning with her two boys, rejoicing that they had asked and found peace in believing. Some people may say that she was a fanatic for going all the way from London to Dundee with her boys to get a blessing.

But last Friday she told me, "My boy who found the Lord in Dundee died three weeks ago." And as she shook my hand as I left the meeting, I said to myself, "Was it not a good thing that mother took her boy to Dundee?" My friends, let us be serious about the salvation of our children and of our friends. Warn that young lady. Yes, mother, speak to that daughter of yours. Father, speak to that child of yours. Wife, speak to your unconverted husband; husband, speak to your unconverted wife. Do not let a man go out of this place saying, "Nobody cared for my soul." I never saw children whose mother was burdened for them not become anxious for Christ. Oh, may there be many sinners seeking the kingdom of God with all their heart!

Before I close, I want to ask you once more what you are going to do. If the Lord is near, won't you call on Him? Don't let that scoffing man next to you keep you out of the kingdom of God. There is a scornful look on that man's face; perhaps he is making fun of what I am saying. Don't mind him; don't look to him. Just look right up to God and ask Him to save you.

Now, every true friend – and you all have friends – every true friend, if you could get his advice tonight, would tell you to be saved now. Ask that minister sitting next you, "Should I seek the kingdom of God tonight?" What does he tell you? "By all means, don't put it off another minute." Ask that godly, praying mother by your side, "Is it best to seek the kingdom of God tonight?" Does she say, "Put it off one week or put it off one month"? Do you think that mother would say that? There is not a Christian mother in this hall who would say it. I doubt if there is even an unconverted mother here whose advice would be to put off becoming a Christian. Ask that praying sister of yours, ask that praying brother, ask any friend you have here – if you are sitting near one – whether it is the very best thing you can do. And then cry up to heaven and ask Him who is sitting at the right hand of God and who loves you more than your father or your mother or anyone on earth – who loves you so much that He gave Himself for you; ask *Him* what He wants you to do and hear His voice from the throne, *"Seek first the kingdom of God"* (Matthew 6:33).

And then shout down to the infernal regions and ask those down there. What will they say? "Send someone to my father's house, *for I have five brothers, that he may testify to them, lest they also come to this place of torment"* (Luke 16:27-28). Heaven, earth, and hell unite in this one thing, *"Seek first the kingdom of God."* Don't put it off. *Call upon Him while He is near.* And if you call on Him earnestly, He will hear that call.

*Oh, may there be many sinners seeking the kingdom of God with all their heart!*

You may call too late. I have no doubt that those who would not pray when the ark was being built prayed when the flood came, but their prayer was not answered. I have no doubt that when Lot left Sodom, Sodom cried to God, but it was too late, and God's judgment swept them from the earth. My friends, it is not too late now, but it may be at twelve o'clock tonight. I cannot find any place in this Bible where I can say you may call tomorrow. I am not justified in saying that. *Behold, now is the accepted time; behold, now is the day of salvation* (2 Corinthians 6:2). Those men of Jerusalem had a golden opportunity with Christ in their midst. We see the Son of God weeping over Jerusalem, His heart bursting with grief for the city, as He cried, *"O Jerusalem, Jerusalem, the one who kills the prophets and stones those who are sent to her! How often I wanted to gather your children together, as a hen gathers her chicks under her wings, but you were not willing!"* (Matthew 23:37). He could look forward forty years and see Titus coming with his army and besieging that city. The Jews called on God then, but it was too late, and over one million people perished. Tonight is a time of mercy.

Perhaps I am talking to someone tonight whose days of grace are few, to someone who may be snatched away very soon. There may be someone here tonight who may never hear another gospel sermon, someone who may be hearing *the last call.* My friend, be wise tonight. Make up your mind that you will seek the kingdom of God now. *Behold, now is the accepted time; behold, now is the day of salvation.* Christ is inviting you to come. *"Come to Me, all you who labor and are heavy laden, and I will give you rest"* (Matthew 11:28). May we all find rest in Christ tonight! Do not let anything divert your mind. This night, this hour, make up your mind that you will not leave this hall until the great question of eternity has been settled.

# WHAT DO YOU THINK ABOUT THE CHRIST?

*Jesus asked them, saying, "What
do you think about the Christ?"*
– Matthew 22:42

I doubt there is anyone here who has not thought about Christ.
You have heard about Him and read about Him and heard
men preach about Him. For eighteen hundred years, men have
been talking about Him and thinking about Him. Some have
their minds made up about who He is, and doubtless, some
have not. And although all these years have passed, this question comes up addressed to each of us today, *"What do you
think about the Christ?"*

I believe this is a proper question to ask one another. If
I were to ask you what you think of any of your prominent
men, you would already have your mind made up about him.
If I were to ask you what you think of your queen, you would
speak right out and tell me your opinion in a minute. If I were
to ask about your prime minister, you would tell me freely what
you had for or against him. Why should people not make up
their minds about the Lord Jesus Christ and take their stand

for or against Him? If you think well of Him, why not speak well of Him and join His side? And if you think poorly of Him, believe He is an impostor, and that He did not die to save the world, why not lift your voice and say you are against Him? It would be a happy day for Christianity if men would just take sides – if we could know positively who was really for Him and who was against Him.

It is of very little importance what the world thinks of anyone else. The king, politicians, and celebrities will soon be gone. It matters relatively little what we think of them. Their lives can only interest a few; but every living soul on the face of the earth is concerned with this Man. The question for the world is, *"What do you think about the Christ?"* I do not ask you what you think of the Presbyterians or the Baptists or the Roman Catholics. I do not ask you what you think of this minister or that, of this doctrine or that; but I want to ask you what you think of the living person of Christ.

I would like to ask if He was really the *Son of God* – the great God-man? Did He leave heaven and come down to this world for a purpose? Was it really to seek and to save? I would like to begin with the manger and follow Him through the thirty-three years He was here on earth. I would ask you what you think of His coming into this world and being born in a manger when it might have been a palace; why He left the grandeur and the glory of heaven and the royal retinue of angels; why He passed by palaces and crowns and dominion and came down here alone?

I would like to ask what you think of Him as a *teacher.* He spoke as no one else had ever spoken (John 7:46). I would like to look at Him as a preacher. I would like to bring you to that mountainside so that we might listen to the words as they fall from His gentle lips. Talk about the preachers of the present day! I would a thousand times rather be five minutes at the feet of Christ than listen a lifetime to all the wise men in the world.

He hung truth on anything. He took a farmer, a fox, a bird, and He gathered the truth around them, so that you cannot see a fox, a farmer, or a bird without thinking what Jesus said. There is a lily of the valley; you cannot see it without thinking of His words, *"They neither toil nor spin"* (Matthew 6:28). He makes the little sparrow chirping in the air preach to us. How fresh those wonderful sermons are, how they live today! How we love to tell them to our children, how the children love to hear! We often hear: "Tell me a story about Jesus." How the little ones love His sermons! No storybook in the world will ever interest them like the stories that He told, yet how profound He was. He puzzled the wise men, and the scribes and the Pharisees could never understand Him! Oh, do you not think He was a wonderful preacher?

*Do you not think He was a wonderful preacher?*

I would like to ask you what you think of Him as a *physician*. A man would soon have a reputation as a doctor if he could cure as Christ did. No case was ever brought to Him that He could not master. He just spoke the word, and disease fled before Him. A man covered with leprosy came. *"Lord, if You are willing, You can make me clean,"* he cried (Matthew 8:2). *"I am willing"* said the Great Physician, and in an instant, the leprosy was gone (Matthew 8:3). The world has hospitals for incurable diseases, but there were no incurable diseases with Him.

See Him in the little home in Bethany, binding up the wounded hearts of Martha and Mary, and tell me what you think of Him as a *comforter*. He is a husband to the widow and a father to the fatherless. The weary may find a resting place on that breast, and the friendless may count Him their friend. He never changes, He never fails, He never dies. His sympathy is ever fresh, His love is always free. O widow and orphans, O sorrowing and mourning, will you not thank God for Christ the comforter?

But these are not the points I wish to look at. Let us go to those who knew Christ and ask what they thought of Him. If you want to find out what a man is today, you inquire about him from those who know him best. I do not wish to be partial; we will go to His enemies and to His friends. We will ask both what they think of the Christ. If we only went to those who liked Him, you would say, "Oh, he is so blind; he thinks so much of the man that he can't see His faults. You can't get anything out of him unless it is in His favor; it is a one-sided affair altogether." So we will go in the first place to His enemies, to those who hated Him, persecuted Him, cursed and killed Him. I will put you in the jury box and call on them to tell us what they think of Him.

First among the witnesses, let us call on the Pharisees. We know how they hated Him. Let us put a few questions to them. Come, Pharisees, tell us what you have against the Son of God. What do *you* think of Christ? Hear what they said! *"This man receives sinners"* (Luke 15:2). What an argument to bring against Him! Why, it is the very thing that makes us love Him. It is the glory of the gospel. He receives sinners. If He had not, what would have become of *us*? Have you nothing more to bring against Him than *this*? Why, it is one of the greatest compliments that was ever paid Him.

Once more, when He was hanging on the tree, you had this to say of Him, *"He saved others; Himself He cannot save"* (Matthew 27:42). He did save others, but He could not save Himself and save us too. So He laid down His own life for yours and mine. Yes, Pharisees, you have told the truth for once in your lives! *He saved others.* He died for others. He was a ransom for many (Mark 10:45); so, it is quite true what you think of Him – *He saved others; Himself He cannot save.*

Now, let us call on Caiaphas. Let him stand up here in his flowing robes, and let us ask him for his evidence. Caiaphas, you were chief priest when Christ was tried. You were president of the Sanhedrin. You were in the council chamber when they found Him guilty; you yourself condemned Him. Tell us, what did the witnesses say? On what grounds did you judge Him? What testimony was brought against Him?

*"He has spoken blasphemy,"* said Caiaphas. *"He said, 'Hereafter you will see the Son of Man sitting at the right hand of the Power, and coming on the clouds of heaven.'* When I heard that, I found Him guilty of blasphemy. I tore my clothes and condemned Him to death" (Matthew 26:64-66). Yes, all that they had against Him was that He was the Son of God, and they killed Him for the promise of His coming for His bride.

Now, let us summon Pilate. Let him enter the witness box. Pilate, this man was brought before you. You examined Him. You talked with Him face to face. What do you think of the Christ? *"I find no fault in this Man,"* said Pilate. "He said He was the King of the Jews" (just as he wrote it over the cross); "but I find no fault in Him" (Luke 23:3-4). Such is the testimony of the man who examined Him! And as he stands there in the center of a Jewish mob, there came a man, elbowing his way, in haste. He rushed up to Pilate and, thrusting out his hand, gave him a message. He tore it open; his face turned pale as he read: *"Have nothing to do with that just Man, for I have suffered many things today in a dream because of Him"* (Matthew 27:19). It was from Pilate's wife – her testimony to Christ. You want to know what His enemies thought of Him? You want to know what a pagan thought? Well, here it is: *"I find no fault in this Man"* and the wife of a pagan: *"that just Man."*

And now, look – in comes Judas. He ought to make a good witness. Let us address him. Come, tell us, Judas, what do you think of Christ? You knew the Master well. You sold Him for thirty pieces of silver; you betrayed Him with a kiss. You saw Him perform those miracles; you were with Him in Jerusalem. In Bethany, when He called up Lazarus, you were there. What do you think about Him? I can see him as he comes into the presence of the chief priests; I can hear the money ring as he throws it on the table. *"I have sinned by betraying innocent blood"* (Matthew 27:4). Here is the man who betrayed Him, and this is what he thinks of Him! Yes, my friends, God has made every man who had anything to do with the death of His Son put their testimony on record that He was an innocent Man.

Look at the centurion who was present at the execution. He was in charge of the Roman soldiers. He had told them to make Him carry His cross; he had given orders for the nails to be driven into His feet and hands, for the spear to be thrust in His side. Let the centurion come forward. Centurion, you had charge of the executioners; you saw that the order for His death was carried out. You saw Him die. You heard Him speak on the cross. Tell us, *what do you think about the Christ?* Look at him. He is striking his breast as he cried, *"Truly, this was the Son of God!"* (Matthew 27:54).

I might go to the thief on the cross and ask what he thought of Him. At first, he railed on Him and reviled Him. But then he thought better of it. *"This Man has done nothing wrong,"* he said (Luke 23:41). I might go further. I might summon the very devils themselves and ask them for their testimony. Have they anything to say of Him? Why, the very devils called Him the Son of God! In Mark, the unclean spirit cried, *"Jesus, Son of the Most High God"* (Mark 5:7). Men say, "Oh, I believe Christ is the Son of God, and because I believe it intellectually, I will be saved." I tell you; the devils did that. And they did more than that, they trembled (James 2:19).

Now let us bring in His friends. We want you to hear their evidence. Let us call that prince of preachers, the forerunner, the wilderness preacher, John. No one except the Master Himself preached like this man. This man drew all Jerusalem and all Judea into the wilderness to hear him; this man burst on the nations like the flash of a meteor. Let John the Baptist come with his leather belt and his camel's hair coat and let him tell us what he thinks of Christ. His words, though they were echoed in the wilderness of Palestine, are written in the Book forever, *"Behold! The Lamb of God who takes away the sin of the world!"* (John 1:29). This is what John the Baptist thought of Him. *"I have seen and testified that this is the Son of God"* (John 1:34). No wonder he drew all Jerusalem and Judea to him, because he preached Christ. And whenever men preach Christ, they are sure to have plenty of followers.

Let us bring in Peter, who was with Him on the Mount of Transfiguration and who was with Him the night He was betrayed. Come, Peter, tell us what you think of Christ. Stand in this witness box and testify of Him. You denied Him once. You said, with a curse, you did not know Him. Was it true, Peter? Don't you know Him?

"Know Him!" l can imagine Peter saying, "It was a lie I told them. I *did* know Him." Afterward, I can hear him charging these Jerusalem sinners with their guilt. He called Him *"both Lord and Christ."* Such was the testimony on the day of Pentecost. *"God has made this Jesus, whom you crucified, both Lord and Christ"* (Acts 2:36). And tradition tells us that when they came to execute Peter, he felt he was not worthy to die in the way his Master died, so he requested to be crucified with his head downward. So much did Peter think of Him!

Now let us hear from the beloved disciple John. He knew more about Christ than any other man. He had laid his head on his Savior's bosom. He had heard the throbbing of that loving heart. Look into his gospel if you wish to know what he thought of Him.

Matthew wrote of Him as the Royal King who had come from His throne. Mark wrote of Him as the Servant, and Luke wrote of Him as the Son of Man. John picked up his pen and, with one stroke, forever settled the question of Unitarianism. He went back before the time of Adam. *In the beginning was the Word, and the Word was with God, and the Word was God* (John 1:1). Look into Revelation. He called Him *the Bright and Morning Star* (Revelation 22:16). So John thought well of Him – because he knew him well.

We might bring in Thomas, the doubting disciple. You doubted Him, Thomas? You would not believe He had risen, and He told you to put your fingers into the wound in His side. What do you think of Him? *"My Lord and my God!"* said Thomas.

Then go over to Decapolis, and you will find Christ has been there casting out devils. Let us call the men of that country and ask what they think of Him. *"He has done all things well,"* they said (Mark 7:37).

But we have other witnesses to bring in. First, the persecuting Saul, once one of the worst of His enemies. Breathing out threats, he met Him. *"Saul, Saul, why are you persecuting Me?"* said Christ (Acts 9:4); and He might have added, "What have I done to you? Have I injured you in any way? Did I not come to bless you? Why do you treat Me this way, Saul?"

And then Saul asked, *"Who are You, Lord?"*

*"I am Jesus, whom you are persecuting"* (Acts 9:5). You see, He was not ashamed of his name. Although He had been in heaven, He said, *"I am Jesus, whom you are persecuting."* What a change that one interview made to Paul! A few years later, we hear him say, *I have suffered the loss of all things, and count them as rubbish, that I may gain Christ* (Philippians 3:8). Such a testimony to the Savior!

But I will go further. I will go away from earth into the other world. I will summon the angels and ask what they think of Christ. They saw Him in the bosom of the Father before the world was. Before the dawn of creation, before the morning stars sang together, He was there. They saw Him leave the throne and come down to the manger. What a scene for them to witness! Ask these heavenly beings what they thought of Him then. For once, they were permitted to speak; for once, the silence of heaven was broken. Listen to their song on the plains of Bethlehem: *"Behold, I bring you good tidings of great joy which will be to all people. For there is born to you this day in the city of David a Savior, who is Christ the Lord"* (Luke 2:10-11). He left the throne to save the world. Is it surprising that the angels thought well of Him?

Then, there are the redeemed saints – those who see Him face to face. Here on earth, He was never known, no one really seemed to be acquainted with Him; but He was known in that world where He had been from the foundation. What do they think of Him there? If we could hear from heaven, we would hear a shout that would glorify and magnify His name. We are told that when John was in the Spirit on the Lord's Day, he heard a shout around him, *ten thousand times ten thousand, and thousands of thousands* of voices saying, *"Worthy is the Lamb who was slain to receive power and riches and wisdom, and strength and honor and glory and blessing!"* (Revelation 1:10; 5:11-12). Yes, He is worthy of all this. Heaven cannot speak too well of Him. Oh, I wish earth would take up the echo and join with heaven in singing, *"Worthy is the Lamb who was slain to receive power and riches and wisdom, and strength and honor and glory and blessing!"*

But there is another witness, even higher than these. Some think that the God of the Old Testament is the Christ of the New. But when Jesus came out of Jordan, baptized by John, there came a voice from heaven. God the Father spoke. It was His testimony to Christ: *"This is My beloved Son, in whom I am well pleased"* (Matthew 3:17). God the Father thinks well of the Son. And if God is well pleased with Him, we should be too. If the sinner and God are well pleased with Christ, then the sinner and God can meet. The moment you say as the Father said, "I am well pleased with Him" and accept Him, you are wedded to God. Will you not believe the testimony? Will you not believe this witness, this last of all, the Lord of hosts, the King of kings Himself?

He repeated it once more so that all may know it. With Peter, James, and John on the Mount of Transfiguration, He cried again, *"This is My beloved Son in whom I am well pleased. Hear Him!"* (Matthew 17:5). And that voice went echoing and re-echoing through Palestine, through all the earth from sea to sea. That voice is echoing still, *Hear Him! Hear Him!*

My friend, will you hear Him today? What is He saying to you? *"Come to Me, all you who labor and are heavy laden, and I will give you rest. Take My yoke upon you and learn from Me, for I am gentle and lowly in heart, and you will find rest for your souls. For My yoke is easy and My burden is light"* (Matthew 11:28-30). Will you think well of such a Savior? Will you believe in Him? Will you trust Him with all your heart and mind? Will you live for Him? If He laid down His life for us, is it not the least we can do to lay down ours for Him? If He bore the Cross and died on it for me, should I not be willing to take it up for Him? We have reason to think well of Him. Do you think it is right and noble to lift your voice against such a Savior? Do you think it is just to cry, "Crucify Him! Crucify Him!" May God help all of us to glorify the Father by thinking well of His only begotten Son!

# EXCUSES - PART I

*"But they all with one accord began to make
excuses. The first said to him, 'I have bought a piece
of ground, and I must go and see it. I ask you to
have me excused.' And another said, 'I have bought
five yoke of oxen, and I am going to test them. I ask
you to have me excused.' Still another said, 'I have
married a wife, and therefore I cannot come.'"*
– Luke 14:18-20

A s soon as anyone begins to preach the gospel, men and
women begin *to make excuses*. It is an old story. There is
not an unsaved person here who does not have some excuse. If
I were to go to each of you and ask why you do not accept God's
invitation to the gospel feast, you would have an excuse ready
on the tip of your tongue; and if you did not have one ready,
the devil would be there to help you make one. And if those
excuses could be answered, he is ready to make new ones. He
has thousands of years of experience, and he is very good at it;
he can give you as many as you want.

Do you know the origin of excuses? You will find it way back in Eden. When Adam had sinned, he tried to excuse himself. *"The woman whom You gave to be with me, she gave me of the tree, and I ate"* (Genesis 3:12). He tried to lay the blame on God, and Eve tried to lay it on the serpent; and from then until now, men and women, with one accord, make excuses.

Remember that the men Luke tells us about were not invited to a funeral or to hear some dry, foolish lecture or sermon; they were not invited to visit a hospital, a prison, or a madhouse. They were not to witness some terrible scene or execution – something that would have pained them. It was to go to a feast. The gospel is represented in the Bible as a feast. In the evening of this age, there is going to be the marriage supper of God's Son. Blessed are those who will be at the marriage supper of the Lamb. If I know my own heart, I would rather be torn limb from limb or have my heart taken from my body this moment and be present on that glorious day than to have the wealth of the world laid at my feet and miss that wonderful banquet at the marriage of the Lamb.

This was not just a feast; it was *a royal feast.* If you had the honor of an invitation from Windsor Castle – if the queen invited you to some great banquet in honor of her son, there is not a man or woman here who would not accept the invitation. You would all want it to be put in the news to show how you were honored. But here is something worth more than that. Here is an invitation from the King of kings, the Lord of lords, God's only Son. Soon He will take His bride into the bridal chamber. The marriage supper of the Lamb is soon approaching. He has gone to prepare new mansions for His bride; the old mansions are not good enough. Then He will come to take her to Himself. It is an invitation to this feast that I bring you. The invitations are going out now to every corner of the earth. There is not one here who is not invited. For eighteen hundred years, God's messengers have been crossing over valley and mountain, over desert and sea, from end to end of the earth, inviting men and women to the gospel feast. What an honor for worms of the dust! When man prepares a feast, there is a great rush to see who will get the best place. But when God prepares His feast, the chairs would all be empty if His disciples did not go out and compel people to come in.

When man prepares a feast, he invites his friends, those who love him; but God invites His bitterest enemies, those who are in rebellion against Him. And still men make excuses! No sooner is the invitation given by God than the excuses begin to pour in.

Did you ever stop to think what would take place if God would take everyone who makes excuses at his word? What if He were to say, "Yes, if you want to be excused from this feast, I will excuse you" and with the next stroke would sweep them all from the face of the earth? Supposing everyone in this country would be taken at their word and laid in the arms of death, how many of your shops would be closed tomorrow? How many homes would be filled with mourning and tears? Not a bar owner would be left to carry on his business; every rum seller wants to be excused. He knows that if he accepts this invitation, he would have to give up his hellish trade. He could not go on making all those fatherless children and taking the bread out of the mouth of the orphan and the widow and be on his way to the marriage supper of the Lamb at the same time. Every bar owner and every drunk wants to be excused. If God *did* excuse them and take them away with a stroke, you would have no drunks reeling through your streets. There would be no harlots then, for every harlot wants to be excused. She knows she has to give up her sins if she wants to be present at the supper of the Lamb. And your wealthier merchants, many of

*No sooner is the invitation given by God than the excuses begin to pour in.*

them, would be gone. They do not want to accept the invitation because they think if they do, they cannot make money as fast. They are carrying on some business that would then have to be stopped, and so they begin to make excuses. But my friends, it would be a somber time if God would take men at their word. The grass would soon be growing in the streets, and the living would be occupied in burying the dead.

Be honest with God today. God is honest; He means what He says. This is an honest invitation, and He wants us to be honest. If you do not want to be at this supper, why not say so? Why make excuses? They are nothing but lies. Is there any one of you who can stand and give a reasonable excuse? If so, tell us why you do not accept this invitation. Think for a minute. What valid reason can you give? You have none. It is not often we get an invitation to attend a royal feast, but here comes one to be present at the marriage supper of God's only Son. It is utter foolishness for anyone to refuse.

Just think what you are asking to be excused from. From heaven, from the fellowship of the pure, from those who have washed their robes in the blood of the Lamb. Man asks to be excused from the mansions that Christ has prepared, from the society of the angels, from God the Father, Christ the Son, and the Holy Spirit. All the really great men of the world are not down here; they are in heaven. You talk of the great men in England, but I tell you the best this earth has ever had are there, and the best that ever lived will be gathered at that feast. For thousands of years, they have been gathering there – all the pure of the earth – Abraham, Isaac, and Jacob. Yes, we will sit down with the patriarchs and prophets, the apostles and martyrs, and with the best that have lived on this earth. I would rather die tonight and be sure of enjoying the bliss of the purified in the world of light than live for centuries with the wealth of this world at my feet and miss the marriage supper of the Lamb. I have missed many appointments in my life, but, by the grace of God, I mean to make sure of that one. Who would miss the blessed privilege of sitting down at the marriage supper of the Lamb, seeing the King in His beauty, and living forever with the Lord?

Let us look at these three men who, *with one accord began to make excuses.*

What did the first one say? *"I have bought a piece of ground, and I must go and see it"* (Luke 14:18). Why did he not go look at the land before he bought it? If he had been a good business-man, he would have seen his ground *first;* he could not make the bargain any better by looking at it now. And now that he has it, he can go look at it anytime; the land will not run away! It was not that he had made a bid and might withdraw or that someone might step in ahead of him and get the land from him. He did not even have that excuse. He had bought the land; there was no fear that he would lose his title to it. Yet he said he needed to go see it. Strange time to go and see ground – just at dinnertime! On the face of it, it was a downright lie. He did not want to go to the feast, so he manufactured this excuse to ease his conscience. That is what people make excuses for. The devil gets men into that cradle and rocks them to sleep in it.

What did the second man say? *"I have bought five yoke of oxen, and I am going to test them. I ask you to have me excused"* (Luke 14:19). Why not test them before he bought them? It is no time to prove oxen after they are bought. And now that the bargain was closed, he could test them at any time. Why not let them stand in the stall until he had accepted this invitation? Do you not see that was another lie?

The third man's excuse was the most ridiculous of them all. *"I have married a wife, and therefore I cannot come"* (Luke 14:20). Why did he not take his wife along with him? Who likes to go to a feast better than a young bride? He could have asked her to go too; if she were not willing, then let her stay at home. The fact was, he did not want to go.

Eighteen hundred years have rolled away, and they tell us the world has grown wiser. They say it has improved wonderfully during these years, but tell me, do people have any better excuses? Young lady! Can you give a better excuse? Do you have an excuse that will stand the light of eternity, an excuse that will even satisfy yourself? Men try every kind of excuse, but there is not a person alive who can give a good one. If a man has a terrible disease and death comes and looks him in the face, his excuses are gone in a moment. My friends, your excuses will look altogether different when you come to stand before the great tribunal of your Judge.

Let us look at some of the popular excuses of the present day. There is one very common one: "I do not like this minister or that pastor." Well, what does that have to do with it? What does the messenger matter? Suppose a boy comes and gives me a message, some good news from my wife. I don't turn around to see who brings it. He may be black or white, fat or skinny, that is nothing to me. It is the message I care about. Is it not the fact that God invites you to a feast? What are you looking at the messenger for? I have heard this excuse until I am tired: "I don't like this minister or that minister, this person or that one who calls himself a Christian." Never mind about the messenger. The question is, are you willing to receive the *message* from God? Do you believe the Word of God is true and that God invites you to this feast? Do you believe that the invitation is to *every creature* in the world (Mark 16:15)? You have nothing to do with the preacher who brings the message. If the message is from God, I ask you, why not accept it? If you are going to wait until you find some perfect man or woman

*Men try every kind of excuse, but there is not a person alive who can give a good one.*

to bring you the invitation, you will never accept it. There was only ever one perfect Man. You will find many flaws in our character, many things you may not like in the followers of Christ, but I challenge you to find a flaw in the character of our Master. *He* tells you to come, and He will receive anyone who accepts the invitation.

I'll tell you of another excuse. Just the other night, a lady came to me after the service and said, "There are so many things in the Bible I cannot understand." There is no doubt about that. God says that the carnal man cannot understand spiritual things, and the Bible is a spiritual book (1 Corinthians 2:14). How can the unregenerate heart understand the Bible? You say, if it is a sealed book, how am I going to be saved? Well, when God put salvation before the world, He made that very plain. The Word of God may be darkened to the natural man, but the way of salvation is written so plainly that a little child of six years old can understand it if she wants. Take this passage and see if you do not understand it: *The Spirit and the bride say, "Come!" And let him who hears say, "Come!" And let him who thirsts come* (Revelation 22:17). Many of you are thirsty. God says come. *Whoever desires, let him take the water of life freely* (Revelation 22:17). You know what it is to take a gift; God puts salvation before you as a gift. *He came to His own, and His own did not receive Him. But as many as received Him, to them He gave the right to become children of God* (John 1:11-12). You can understand that. *"Believe on the Lord Jesus Christ, and you will be saved"* (Acts 16:31). You know what it is to believe. At any rate, you know what it is to trust, to commit your soul to the Lord Jesus Christ – that is all.

There are mysterious things in the Bible now, but when you begin to trust Christ, your eyes will be opened, and the Bible will be a new book to you. Many things that are dark and mysterious today will have a new beauty tomorrow. It will become the Book of books to you. Today Christ may be *a root out of dry ground*, without *form or comeliness* (Isaiah 53:2), but He will become to you the *chief among ten thousand*, the *altogether lovely* (Song of Solomon 5:10, 16), *the Bright and Morning Star* (Revelation 22:16) if you trust Him as your Savior. Then you will understand the Bible.

No book in the world has been so misjudged as the Bible. People judge it without even reading it, or perhaps they read a bit here and a bit there and then close it saying, "It is so dark and mysterious!" If you were to read a book and someone asks you what you think about it, you would say, "I have only read it through once and not very carefully, so I cannot really give an opinion." Yet people pick up God's book, read a few pages, and condemn the whole thing. Of all the skeptics and unbelievers I have ever met speaking against the Bible, I have never met one who read it through. There may be such men, but I have never met them. It is simply an excuse. There is no man alive who will stand up before God and say that kept him out of the kingdom. It is the devil trying to make us believe it is not true and that it is dark and mysterious. The only way to overcome the great enemy of souls is by the written Word of God. He knows that, and so he tries to make men not believe it. As soon as a man is a true believer in the Word of God, he is a conqueror over Satan.

Young man! The Bible is true. What have these unbelievers to give you in its place? What has made England but the open Bible? Every nation that exalts the Word of God is exalted, and every nation that casts it down is cast down. Oh, cling close to the Bible. Of course, we will not understand it all at once, but men are not to condemn it on that account. Suppose I should send my little five-year-old boy to school tomorrow morning, and when he came home in the afternoon, I say to him, "Willie, can you read? Can you write? Can you spell? Do you understand all about algebra, geometry, Hebrew, Latin, and Greek?"

"Why, Papa," the little fellow would say, "how funny you talk; I have been trying all day to learn the ABCs!"

Well, suppose I should reply, "If you have not finished your education, you do not need to go anymore." What would you say? Why, you would say I had gone mad. There would be just about as much reason in that as in the way that people talk about the Bible. My friends, the men who have studied the Bible for fifty years – the wise men and the scholars, the great theologians – have never gotten to the depths of it. There are truths there that the church of God has been searching out for the last eighteen hundred years, but no man has fathomed the depths of that ever-living stream.

There is another group here who says, "That's not my difficulty. I believe the Word of God. But if I could speak alone with you, I would tell you my excuse. The truth is that I love the world very much, and if I become a Christian, I will have to give up all pleasure and go through the world sad and never smile again. My joy will be forever gone!" Well, I want to say that no greater lie was ever forged than that. The devil started it way back in Eden, but there is not one word of truth in it. It is a libel on Christianity. It does *not* make a man gloomy to become a child of God. Imagine a man about to be executed. In a few moments, he will be launched into eternity. But suddenly a message comes: he is reprieved. I quickly run to the man. I shout, "Good news! Good news! You are *not* to die!" Does that make him gloomy? No! No! No! Young men, young women, old and young, don't believe Satan's lies any longer. It is not having Christ that makes men gloomy. If you give water to someone who is really thirsty, dying for lack of water, is that going to make him gloomy? That is what Christ is – water to the thirsty soul. If a man is dying for lack of bread and you give him bread, will that make him gloomy? That is what Christ is to the soul – the bread of life. You will never have true pleasure, peace, joy, or comfort until you have found Christ.

The idea that a Christian cannot have peace and joy in this world is foolishness. That used to be my difficulty. But I want to tell you I had more joy, comfort, and peace the first year after I was converted than I had all my previous life put together, and I never heard of any young convert who would not testify the same thing.

Another excuse – there are so many of them! The air is full of them. I hear someone say, "Well, I would like to be a Christian, but it is a very hard thing. I have tried it many times. I do not want to be blunt, but that is just the honest truth." I will tell you what you have been doing; you have been trying to serve God with the old carnal mind. You might as well try to walk to the moon! It is utterly impossible. The Ethiopian cannot change his skin; the leopard cannot change its spots (Jeremiah 13:23). It is impossible to serve God with the old carnal heart; but with a new heart, God will give you the power, and then you will not talk about it being hard to serve Him. That is just another lie.

Let us look at that. Do you mean to say that God is a hard master? Do you say it is a hard thing to serve God? Do you say that Satan is an easy master, and that it is easier to serve him than God? Is it honest – is it true? God a hard master! If I read my Bible right, I read that *the way of the unfaithful is hard* (Proverbs 13:15). It is the devil who is the hard master. Yes, the way of the unfaithful is hard. The Word of God cannot be changed. If you doubt it, young man, look at the convict in the prison, right in the prime of life. He has been there for ten years and must remain for ten years more – twenty years taken out of his life. When he comes out of that miserable cell, he comes out a branded felon! Do you think *that* man will tell you, "The way of the unfaithful has been easy"? Go ask the poor drunk, the man who is bound hand and foot, the slave of the infernal cup, who is rushing toward a drunkard's hell. Ask him if he has found the way of the unfaithful easy. "Easy?" he will cry. "Easy?" The way of the unfaithful is hard and gets harder and harder every day! Go ask the immoral person and the person who loves the world's pleasures; go ask the gambler and the blasphemer – with one voice they will tell you that the service has been hard. Take the most faithful follower of the devil and put him on this platform tonight and let us ask him. The best way to settle this question is to find out by the testimony of those that have served both masters. I do not think a man has any right to judge until he has served both. If I heard a man condemn a master, I would ask if he had served him; if he had not, he could not very well testify.

*I want to stand here tonight as a witness for Christ.*

But if you have served two masters, then you are very good judges. I want to stand here tonight as a witness for Christ. I have been in His school for twenty years, and I want to testify tonight that I have found Him an easy master. I used to say, as you do, that it is a hard thing to be a Christian, and I thought it was. But now I tell you that the yoke is easy, and the burden is light. And I am speaking to many more tonight who have served both masters. Many of you have served Christ, and many of you, before you were brought into His fold, served the devil. I would like to ask you, you who are Christ's, you who have served Him – some five, some ten, some twenty years – is Jesus a hard master? I hear your shouts of "No! No!" I thought you would say that. I knew that you would. I never heard a man say, "I have served Christ for five years or for ten and found Him a hard master." Now let me put you into the witness box again. For many years you served Satan; some of you are serving him still. Do you find him to be a hard master? "Yes!" you say. Yes, my friends, you cannot help admitting it. You *know* it is true: *the way of the unfaithful is hard.*

Suppose we could go beyond this life; suppose we could go down to the bottomless pit and summon Judas, who has been there for the last eighteen hundred years. Suppose we say, Judas, you betrayed the Son of God, sold Him for thirty pieces of silver. You have served the devil faithfully; have you found his service an easy one? What a wail would rise from those lips! Do you think Judas found it easy? Do you think he found Satan a kind master? He threw down the thirty pieces of silver! Why, he was so tired of the devil's service that he hanged himself twenty-four hours after publicly entering it.

Now let us call on Paul who, you may say, took the place that Judas once filled. Let him come down from the hilltops of glory. Do you think he would say it was a hard thing to serve God and an easy thing to serve the devil? "I served the devil well," he says. "I breathed out threats, I persecuted the church, but it was hard for me to kick against the goads" (Acts 9:1, 5).

And now let us see what God says about it. I would like to ask those who think He is a hard master what they would do with a passage like this, *"Come to Me, all you who labor and are heavy laden, and I will give you rest. Take My yoke upon you and learn from Me, for I am gentle and lowly in heart, and you will find rest for your souls. For My yoke is easy and My burden is light"* (Matthew 11:28-30). Yes, it is an easy thing to serve someone we love. If you love a person, you are delighted to please them!

My friends, do not dishonor God by calling Him a hard master. Speak to the young disciple of the Lord Jesus. Look at his face. See how his eyes are lit with a light from heaven, how the glow from Calvary is shed around his path. Let him tell of the peace and the joy he has found in the service of Christ. Let him tell, until language fails him, how the way grows lighter and lighter as he journeys on, how his hopes grow brighter and brighter as he nears his eternal home. Oh, yes, there is a vast difference in the yoke of Satan and the yoke of Christ. The yoke of the Christian is easy and light; the yoke of the devil is heavy and hard. I beg of you, do not listen to Satan's lies. He has deceived the whole human race. Oh, change masters tonight and accept the invitation to be present at the marriage supper of the Lamb.

# EXCUSES - PART 2

*"But they all with one accord began to make excuses. The first said to him, 'I have bought a piece of ground, and I must go and see it. I ask you to have me excused.' And another said, 'I have bought five yoke of oxen, and I am going to test them. I ask you to have me excused.' Still another said, 'I have married a wife, and therefore I cannot come.'"*
– Luke 14:18-20

The next excuse I want to look at is election. I meet many who tell me they are very anxious to be saved, but they do not know if they are elected. "If I were only sure that I were elected," they say, "I would soon be serious about salvation. But then I don't know that I'm one of the elect, so I have a very good excuse." Now I want to be clear on this point. I want to say that an unconverted person has nothing whatever to do with the doctrine of election. After you have become children of God, then we can talk about election – then we can talk about how sweet and beautiful the doctrine is. But those who are not God's children have nothing at all to do with it. You do not like anyone to read your private letters, do you? Well, the doctrine of election was written, in a private letter, to the children of God. No wonder the world puzzles over it. No wonder they cannot understand it. It was never meant for them. What they have to do with is the *whoever* and the *one who comes to Me* of the free invitations of Christ.

Suppose I am taking a walk near this hall tonight and say to the policeman at the door, "Who is invited to this meeting?"

"Those who have tickets," he replies. I have no ticket, so it is not for me. I walk on further and come to another meeting.

"This is only for those belonging to the society," I am told, so I know it is not for me. I go on further and come to a large public building – a club.

"Only members admitted," I read at the door. It is not for me either. I go further still and come to another building, and over the door this is written: "Whoever will, let him come in." It is for me this time. Whoever – that means me – and in I go. My friends, God puts it just like that. All are invited to come to Christ. What do you have to do with Paul's letter about election? You have nothing to do with it – not until you become a Christian. You have no business with the private letters of other people, and the *whoever* comes before election. If you learn to read, you start with the alphabet, don't you? You don't learn to read all at once. And if you come to Christ, you must come in God's way, and then you can talk about how you came.

But you say there is another side to that. Christ said, *"No one can come to Me unless the Father who sent Me draws him"* (John 6:44). I say Christ *is* drawing men: *"I, if I am lifted up from the earth, will draw all peoples to Myself"* (John 12:32). He is drawing men, but they will not come. God was in Christ reconciling the world to Himself and drawing men to Him. That drawing is going on now, but many hearts are fighting against the effort of the Spirit. God is drawing men heavenward, and the devil is drawing them hellward.

Suppose someone who wished to go to London would say, "I don't know if God has decreed it. If I am to be there, I will be there. Anyhow, it is no use my taking the train. What is the use of my paying the fare and taking the trouble to get on it? If I am elected to get there, I will get there somehow." Who would use such language as that? Or suppose a farmer were to say, "I am not going to plant; if God has decreed that I am to have a crop, I will have it. I am not going to trouble myself tilling the ground or working hard; if God has decreed that I will have a good harvest, I will have it without any tilling." Or suppose you are sick and do not go to the doctor. Suppose you say, "If God has decreed it, I will get well," so you refuse to take the medicine. You say, "There is no point; if God has decreed that I am to get well, I will get well without it." Who talks that way? Yet many people carry out that very doctrine regarding spiritual things.

*God is drawing men heavenward, and the devil is drawing them hellward.*

I think that the Lord Jesus saw how men were going to stumble over this doctrine, so after He had been thirty or forty years in heaven, He came down and spoke to John. One Lord's Day in Patmos, He said to him, "Write these things to the churches." John kept on writing. His pen flew very fast. And then the Lord, when it was nearly finished, said, "John, before you close the book, put this in: *'The Spirit and the bride say, "Come!" And let him who hears say, "Come!"'* But there will be some who are deaf, and they cannot hear, so add, *'Let him who thirsts come.'* And in case there are any who do not thirst, make it broader, *'Whoever desires, let him take the water of life freely'*" (Revelation 1:10-11; 22:17). What more can you have than that?

And the book is sealed, as it were, with that. It is the last invitation in the Bible. *Whoever desires, let him take the water of life freely.* You are thirsty. You want water. I hold out this glass to you and say, "Take it." You say, "If I am decreed to have it, I am not going to go to the trouble of taking it." Well, you will never get it. And if you are ever to have salvation, you must reach out your hand and take it. *I will take up the cup of salvation, and call upon the name of the Lord* (Psalm 116:13). Will you take it tonight? It is simple enough; it is a gift. *The wages of sin is death, but the gift of God is eternal life* (Romans 6:23). My dear friends, do not stumble over the doctrine of election any longer. You will not be able to stand up before God and say, "I did not accept the invitation because I was not one of the elect." That excuse will fade away in His presence. God invites every man and woman to the gospel feast when He writes, *Whoever desires, let him take.*

There is someone else who says, "That is not my difficulty. I know a man who belongs to the professing church of Christ, and he cheated me years ago. There are hypocrites in the church, and I am not going to have anything to do with it. You won't catch me being in the company of hypocrites."

Well, I will find you two hypocrites in the world for every one you will find in the church. Besides, I am not asking you to come to the church – not that I do not believe in churches – but I am asking you to the marriage supper of the Lamb. Come to Christ first, and then we can talk to you about the church. There always have been hypocrites in the church, and there always will be. One of the twelve apostles turned out to be a hypocrite, and there will be hypocrites in the church until the end of time. But there will not be one hypocrite at this feast, and if you want to get out of the company of hypocrites, you had better hurry and come to Christ. If you do not accept the invitation, you will have to spend eternity with them. Even if everyone here were a blackhearted hypocrite, what does that have to do with you? "Follow Me," says Christ. Do not look to John or Peter or Paul, this man or that, but straight to Christ. You may find many flaws in our characters, but you will find none in Christ's. We find many in ourselves, and you may too. But we do not ask you to follow us but Christ. There will be no hypocrites at the marriage supper of the Lamb; they will all be in the lost world. And if you do not accept the invitation, you will have to spend eternity with hypocrites. So, if you really object to them, you need to make sure you have a place at the marriage supper of the Lamb.

But there is a self-righteous Pharisee here who says, "Well, I don't understand all this talk about conversion; I'm good enough as I am. My excuse will stand if the others will not. I am not going to go ask people to pray for me; I don't need it." And he draws his filthy rags of self-righteousness around him and thinks he is pure in the sight of God and man. My friend, the Word of God says, *"There is none righteous, no, not one"* (Romans 3:10). If you are found with your own garment on, you will be cast out from this feast. He will provide you with a robe of spotless white if you will accept it, but you must not think you can stand in the presence of the King with these miserable rags of self-righteousness on you. May the Holy Spirit show you how vile you are in the sight of a holy God. The nearer a man gets to God, the more he abhors himself. When a man is getting near to God, he begins to loathe himself. Like Job, he says, *"I abhor myself"* (Job 42:6). Like Isaiah when he saw the holy God, he cries out, *"Woe is me, for I am undone!"* (Isaiah 6:5). Like that holy man Daniel, his vigor is turned to frailty (Daniel 10:8). May God strip you of your self-righteousness today!

Here is another excuse. If the devil cannot make a man believe he is good enough without being saved, then he will tell him he is so bad that the Lord will have nothing to do with him. Many make that excuse. "I would like to be saved," they say, "but I am too bad." That is another lie. The Scripture says, *Christ died for the ungodly* (Romans 5:6). Jesus Christ came into the world to save sinners. What did Christ say to His disciples?

*"Go into all the world and preach the gospel to every creature* (Mark 16:15), *that repentance and remission of sins should be preached in His name to all nations, beginning at Jerusalem"* (Luke 24:47). God offered salvation to the very men whose hands were dripping with the blood of the Son of God! Paul said he was the chief of sinners (1 Timothy 1:15), and if he was saved, certainly there is hope for every person on the face of the earth. If you are terribly bad, you are the very one He wants to save.

*Do not put these filthy rags of self-righteousness on you.*

During our Civil War, I remember that after the battles were over, the doctor used to go look at the wounded men. He would determine the most desperate cases and attend to them first. That is the way the great Physician does now. He saves the worst men He can get. I know many people who are anxious to come, but they are waiting until they grow a little better. They think God will not take them until then.

Notice, my friends, the Lord invites you to come just as you are, and if you could make yourself better, you would not be any more acceptable to Him. Do not put these filthy rags of self-righteousness on you. God will strip every rag from you when you come to Him and clothe you with glorious garments. When our war was going on, we would sometimes go to the recruiting office and see a man come in with a silk hat, expensive coat, calf-skin boots, and a suit worth one thousand dollars. Another man would come in whose clothes were worth a few dollars; but they both had to strip and put on the uniform of the country. When we enter into Christ's service, we must put on the garments of heaven and be stripped of every rag. No matter how bad you are, come just as you are, and the Lord will receive you.

I read about an artist who wanted to paint a picture of the Prodigal Son. He searched through the madhouses, the poor-houses, and the prisons to find a man wretched enough to represent the prodigal, but he could not find one. One day he was walking down the streets and met a man whom he thought would do. He told the poor beggar he would pay him well if he came to his room and sat for his portrait. The beggar agreed, and they set a time for him to come. The day came, and a man appeared at the artist's room. When he was shown into the studio, the man said, "You made an appointment with me."

The artist looked at him. "I never saw you before," he said; "you cannot have an appointment with me."

"Yes," he said, "I agreed to meet you today at ten o'clock."

"You must be mistaken; it must have been some other artist. I was to see a *beggar* here at this hour."

"Well," said the beggar, "I am he."

"You?"

"Yes."

"Why, what have you been doing?"

"Well, I thought I would dress myself up a bit before I got painted."

"Then," said the artist, "I do not want you. I wanted you *as you were; now*, you are no use to me."

That is the way Christ wants every poor sinner, just as he is. Someone will say, "Oh, but my heart is so hard." Well, that is just the very reason you ought to come. If you did not have a hard heart, you would not need a Savior. Do you think you can soften your heart? Can you break your heart? Did not God invite the hard-hearted? Did not Christ come *to seek and to save that which was lost* (Luke 19:10)? It is because men's hearts are hard that they need a Savior, so that is no excuse at all. God invites you, and you cannot stand up and say to the great King you did not accept the invitation because you had a hard heart. He invites *whoever*, and you can come along with your hard heart just as it is.

Up north, a minister was talking to a man after the service.

"My heart is so hard, it seems as if it were chained, and I cannot come," said the man. The minister said to him, "Come along, chain and all," and he just came to Christ, hard-hearted, chain and all, and Christ snapped the fetters and set him free right there. If you are bound hands and feet by Satan, it is the work of God to break the fetters; you cannot break them. But, thank God, He can snap the fetters of every sin-bound soul tonight and set each captive free.

There is another excuse. "I would like to come, but I do not know that I feel right about it." That is a very common excuse. Feeling, feeling, feeling, feeling! I have heard that cry until I am sick of it. Suppose a friend invites me to dinner today, and I say, "Well, I would like to have dinner with you. There is no one I would rather dine with than you, but I do not know if I feel right."

"Are you sick?" he might ask.

"No, I never felt better in my life."

"Well, what do you mean?"

"I don't know that I feel just right. I do not know that I will be in a right state of mind."

"I do not understand you," he would say. "What do you mean?"

"Well, I would like to go very much, but I don't feel right."

And that is the way men are talking now. "I would like to go to heaven, but I don't know that I have the right kind of feeling." But, my friends, if you really want to, God invites you, and that is all there is to it. My friend urges me to come, but I keep on saying, "I do not know that I am in the right state of mind."

"Why," he would say, "I think Mr. Moody must be out of his mind. I invited him to dinner, and instead of giving me a simple answer, he kept talking about feeling all the time!"

You might laugh, but that is just the way people talk to us – hundreds of them. My friends, is God inviting you? If He is, why don't you accept the invitation? If you want to come, just come along and don't talk about feeling. Do you think Lazarus had any feeling when Christ called him out of the grave?

My friends, God is above feeling. Do you think you can control your feelings? I am sure if I could control my feelings, I would never have any bad feelings, only good. Bear in mind that Satan may change our feelings fifty times a day, but he cannot change the Word of God; and we want to build our hopes of heaven on the Word of God. When a poor sinner is coming up out of the pit, ready to get his feet on the Rock of Ages, the devil sticks out a plank of feeling and says, "Get on that." When the sinner puts his feet on that plank, down he goes again. Look at this text: *"Most assuredly, I say to you, he who hears My word and believes in Him who sent Me has everlasting life, and shall not come into judgment, but has passed from death into life"* (John 5:24).

My friend, that is worth more than all the feelings that you can have in a whole lifetime. I would much rather stand on that verse alone than on all the feelings I ever had. I took my stand there twenty years ago. Since then, the dark waves of hell have come dashing up against me. The waves of persecution have broken all around me; doubts, fears, and unbelief in turn have assailed me, but I have been able to stand firm on this short word of God. It is a sure footing for eternity. It was true eighteen hundred years ago, and it is true tonight. That rock is higher than my feelings. We need to get our feet on the rock, and the Lord will put a new song in our mouths.

But someone else here may say, "He does not know my situation at all. None of these things ever trouble me. The fact is, I cannot believe. I would like to come, but I cannot believe."

Not long ago a man said to me, "I cannot believe."

"Whom?" I asked.

He stammered and said again, "I cannot believe."

I said, "Whom?"

"Well," he said, "I *can't* believe."

"Whom?" I asked again.

At last, he said, "I cannot believe myself."

"Well, you don't need to. You do not need to put any confidence in yourself. The less you believe in yourself the better. But if you tell me that you can't believe God, that is another thing; and I would like to ask you why." If a man says to me, "I respect you. I admire you, but I do not believe a word you say," I say to myself, "I certainly do not think much of your admiration." But that is the way many people talk about God. They say, "I have a profound reverence for God. The very name of God strikes awe in my heart; but I do not believe Him."

Why don't you be honest and say that you *won't* believe? There is no real reason why men cannot believe God. I challenge any unbeliever on the face of the earth to put his finger on one promise God has ever made that He has not kept. The idea of a man standing up at this point in history and saying he cannot believe God! My friend, you have no reason to not believe Him. If you say you cannot believe man, there would be some reason in that because men very often say what is not true. But God never makes any mistakes. *"Has He spoken, and will He not make it good?"* (Numbers 23:19). Believe in God and say as Job says: *"Though He slay me, yet will I trust Him"* (Job 13:15).

Some men talk as if it were a great misfortune that they do not believe. They seem to look on it as a kind of infirmity and think they ought to be sympathized with and pitied. But bear in mind that it is the most damning sin of the world. *"When He* [the Holy Spirit] *has come, He will convict the world of sin, and of righteousness, and of judgment: of sin, because they do not believe in Me"* (John 16:8-9). That is the sin of the world – *they do not believe in Me.* That is the very root of sin; the fruit is bad because the tree is bad. May God open our eyes to see that He is true, and may we all be led to put our fullest trust in Christ.

But you say, "I do not know what it is to believe." That is another excuse. Well, let me put it differently. Suppose I say *trust* Him – just take Him at His word. Believe that He really invites you – that He wants you to come. If you do not know what it is to believe, will you not just trust God?

But another one says, "I would like to believe very much, but I am afraid I would not hold out." Now, I have had a rule for many years that has been a great help to me: never cross a mountain until you come to it. You trust Christ to save you tonight, and perhaps the devil throws a little straw across your path, tries to magnify it, and makes you think it is a great mountain. Never mind the mountains; trust Him tonight to save you. If He can save you tonight, He can keep you tomorrow. When you have sat down at the banquet and had one good feast, when you have had one meeting with Christ, you will not want to leave Him. I accepted this invitation twenty years ago, and I have never wanted to go back. But I could not have kept myself from falling away all these years. I would have fallen in twenty-four hours if it was up to me. But thank God, we do not have to keep ourselves. The Lord is my Keeper – my Shepherd, I shall not want. He keeps us. It takes the same grace to keep us that it does to save us. And God has told us, *"My grace is sufficient for you."*

*That is the very root of sin; the fruit is bad because the tree is bad.*

But some people are not at all afraid of falling away. They are sure that God is quite able to save them and quite strong enough to keep them. But when you ask them if they are Christians, they say, "Well, you know, I would like to be, but I have no time." If I were to go to the door tonight, take you by the hand, and say, "My friend, why not accept the invitation tonight?" some of you would say, "Please excuse me tonight. I really have no time. I have some important business to attend to tomorrow morning, and I must go home as fast as possible to get my night's rest. You really must excuse me." And the mothers would say, "We have to run home and put the children to bed; you must excuse us this time." So thousands and thousands say they have no time to be a Christian. But, my friends, what have you done with all the time that God has given you? What have you been doing all these months and years that have passed since He gave you birth? Is it true you have no time? What did you do with the 365 days of last year? Did you have no time at all during these last twelve months to seek the kingdom of God? You spend twenty years getting an education to enable you to earn a living for this poor frail body, so soon to be eaten by worms. You spend seven or eight years learning a trade so that you may earn your daily bread, yet you do not have five minutes to accept this invitation of Christ's! My friend, bear in mind you will die whether you plan for it or not, and you will at the appointed time stand in the presence of the Judge. And when He calls you to stand before that bar, will you dare to tell Him that you had no time to prepare for the marriage supper of His Son? You have no time? Take time! Let everything else be laid aside until you have accepted this invitation. This excuse is a lie. If you do not have time, make it. *"Seek first the kingdom of God"* (Matthew 6:33). Let the children stay up a little late tonight. Let your business be postponed tomorrow. Maybe you will not make as much money tomorrow, but what does it matter if you get Christ? Better for a man to be sure of salvation than to gain the whole world and lose his own soul (Matthew 16:26).

Maybe you say, "I would like to become a Christian, but I have a problem with these special meetings and Americans and laymen too. If this were a regular service and our regular minister were speaking, I would accept the invitation." If that is your difficulty, I can help you. You can get right up, leave the hall, and walk straight over to your minister and have a talk with him. If you say you do not want to be converted in a special meeting, there are regular meetings in all the churches throughout the town, and your minister would be glad to talk with you about your soul. But if you say, "There is a great awakening here in London, and I do not want to be converted in the time of a revival," you can step onto a train and go to some town where there is no revival. We can find you some place where there is no revival and some church where there is not much of the revival spirit without much difficulty. If you really want to go, don't give that as an excuse.

How wise the devil is! When the church is cold and everything is dead, men say, "Oh, well, if there were only some life in the church, I might become a Christian. If we could only just have a wave of blessing from heaven, it would be so easy then." Then when the wave does come, they say, "Oh, no, we are afraid of excitement and afraid of these special meetings. We are afraid something will be done that won't be in accordance with our ideas of propriety." Oh, my friends, do not listen to these subtle lies. Just come as you are to Christ and accept the offer that He makes you now.

I wish I had time to go on with these excuses, but they are as numerous as the hairs of my head. And if I could go on and try to exhaust them all, the devil would just help you to make more. The best thing you can do is to tie them all into one bundle and stamp them as a pack of lies; not a single one of them is true. God will sweep them all away some day if you do not do it now. It is a very solemn thought that God will excuse you if you want to be excused. He does not wish to do it, but He will do it. *"As I live, says the LORD GOD, I have no pleasure in the death of the wicked, but that the wicked turn from his way and live. Turn, turn from your evil ways! For why should you die, O house of Israel?"* (Ezekiel 33:11). Look at the Jewish nation. They wanted to be excused from the feast. They despised the grace of God and trampled it under foot; look at them today! Yes, it is easy enough to say, "I ask You to have me excused," but soon God may take you at your word and say, "Yes, I will excuse you." While others who have accepted the invitation sit down to the marriage supper of the Lamb amid the shouts and hallelujahs in heaven, you will be crying in the company of the lost, *"The harvest is past, the summer is ended, and we are not saved!"* (Jeremiah 8:20).

Remember, it is the King of kings, the Lord of glory, who invites you to this feast. Come just as you are and accept the invitation. Let the plow stand in the furrow until you have accepted it. Let the shop be closed until then; let business wait until you have accepted it. Let the land rest; let the ox stand in the stall until you have accepted that invitation. Make sure, whatever you do, that you will not be missing from the marriage supper of the Lamb. That wonderful mother of yours, if she had Christ as her Redeemer, will be there. That little child who died a few months ago will be there. Young lady! Do you want to be excused? He will excuse you. Do you want to be excused, young man? He will excuse you. You may make light of it tonight if you choose. "Oh, no," you say, "I never do that. I might have done other things, but I have never done that!" Have you not? Suppose I get an invitation to dinner tomorrow, but I take it and tear it up. I do not answer it; I pay no attention to it. Is that not making light of it? How many of you will go away tonight paying no attention to this invitation? Everyone who goes home unconcerned, won't he be making light of it? The Lord has invited you to the gospel feast. Are you going to spend this evening accepting or making light of the invitation?

God does not want you to die; He wants you to accept this invitation and live. If you have a good excuse, one that will stand the light of eternity, hold on to it. Do not give it up for anything. Take it down with you into the grave. Hold it firm. Take it to where God sits in judgment and tell it to Him. But if you have one that won't stand the test of eternity, give it up. If you have an excuse that will not stand the piercing eye of God, I beg you, as a friend, give it up tonight. Let it go to the four winds of heaven and accept the invitation to be at the marriage supper of the Lamb. Do not let the laughing, scoffing, mocking world laugh your soul into eternal death. Do as the pilgrim did, whom John Bunyan describes as starting out from the City of Destruction crying, "Life! Life! Eternal life!" Set your face like a flint toward that blessed land and say, "By the grace of God, I will be at the marriage supper of the Lamb."

*"By the grace of God, I will be at the marriage supper of the Lamb."*

Suppose we write out here tonight this excuse. How would it sound? *"To the King of Heaven. While sitting here in this hall, in such and such a city and date, I received a very pressing invitation from one of your servants to be present at the marriage supper of your only begotten Son. I ask You to have me excused."* Would you sign that, young man? Would you, mother? Would you come up to this table, pick up a pen, and put your name down on such an excuse? You would say, "Let my right hand forget its skill and my tongue cling to the roof of my mouth if I sign that" (Psalm 137:6). I doubt if there is one here who would sign it. Then pay attention to God's invitation. I beg you not to make light of it. It is a loving God inviting you to a feast, and God is not to be mocked. Go play with the forked lightning, go trifle with pestilence and disease, but do not trifle with God.

Let me write out another answer. *"To the King of Heaven. While sitting in the hall in such and such a city and date, I received a pressing invitation from one of your messengers to be present at the marriage supper of your only begotten Son. I hurry to reply. By the grace of God, I will be present."* Who will sign that? Is there one who will put his name on it? Is there no one who will say, "By the grace of God I will accept the invitation now"? May God bring you to a decision now. If you ever want to see the kingdom of God, you must decide this question one way or the other. What will you do with the invitation? I bring it to you in the name of my Master; will you accept or reject it? Be wise tonight and accept the invitation. Make up your mind that you will not go away until the question of eternity is settled. The prayer of my heart is that God may bring hundreds to a decision tonight.

# THE BLOOD - PART I

*The Old Testament*

*"It is the blood that makes atonement for the soul."*
– Leviticus 17:11

E very person should be able to give a reason for the hope that is in him (1 Peter 3:15); and I do not believe there is anyone alive who is a stranger to the blood who can give a reason for his hope beyond the grave. I am often told that I make the plan of salvation too easy and that it is foolish to say that men can be saved by simply trusting the atoning blood of Christ. Now I do not wish anyone to believe what I say if it is not according to Scripture; the best way is just to open the Bible and see what the Word of God says about it.

I call your attention to the very first book of the Bible. If you turn to Genesis 3:21, you find: *For Adam and his wife the* LORD *God made tunics of skin, and clothed them.* In this verse we get the first glimpse of the blood. Certainly, God could not have clothed Adam and Eve with the skins of animals unless

He had shed blood. And to me it is a very sweet thought that sin was covered before Adam was driven out of Eden – that God dealt in grace with him before He dealt in judgment. It may be that this was a type, way back in Eden, of Christ, the coming One, of the Sacrifice to be slain; and Adam might have said to his wife, "Well, even though God has driven us out of Eden, He loves us, and this coat is a token of His love."

Someone said God put a lamp of promise into Adam's hand before He drove him out: the seed of the woman will bruise the head of the serpent (Genesis 3:15). Did you ever think what a terrible state of things it would be if man, in his lost and ruined state, were allowed to live forever? Because God loved Adam, He drove him out of Eden so that he would not live forever and placed the cherubim there with the flaming sword. But now Christ has come and taken the sword into Himself and opened wide the gates so that man can come in and eat. Adam might have been in Eden ten thousand years and then been led astray by Satan; but now *our life is hidden with Christ in God* (Colossians 3:3). Yes, man is safer with the second Adam out of Eden than with the first Adam in Eden.

Then let us turn to Genesis 4:4: *Abel also brought of the firstborn of his flock and of their fat. And the LORD respected Abel and his offering, but He did not respect Cain and his offering. And Cain was very angry, and his countenance fell.* Here were two boys who were born and brought up outside of Eden. They were children of the same parents and brought up under similar circumstances and under the same influences, and there is no account of any difference between these two boys until they offer a sacrifice. Abel brought the blood and was accepted; Cain came in his own way and was rejected. Undoubtedly, when our first parents fell, God marked out the way by which man might come to Him; Abel walked in God's way, but Cain walked in his own.

You may have wondered why Cain's offering was not just as acceptable to God as Abel's; but one took God's way, and the other took his own. Perhaps Cain said he could not bear the sight of blood and took that which God had cursed and laid it on the altar. Perhaps he said to himself, "I will certainly not bring a bleeding lamb. I don't like that doctrine at all. Here is the grain and the beautiful fruit that I have raised by my own work and effort, and I'm sure it looks better than blood." There are many Cainites in the church today. They are trying to get into heaven their own way. They bring their own good deeds to God. They prefer what is agreeable to the eye, as Cain did his beautiful corn and fruit; but they do not like the doctrine of the blood of the atonement. From the time Adam left Eden, there have been Abelites and Cainites. The Abelites come by way of the blood – the Cainites come in a way of their own. They wish to get rid of the doctrine of the blood. But be assured that any religion that makes light of the blood is of the devil. No matter how eloquent a man is, if he preaches against the blood, he is doing the devil's work. Do not listen to him. Do not believe him. If an angel from heaven would preach any other gospel, I would not believe it. *Christ died for our sins* is the gospel that Paul preached (1 Corinthians 15:3), that Peter preached, and that God has always honored in the salvation of men's souls.

*Any religion that makes light of the blood is of the devil.*

The next glimpse we get of the blood is in Genesis 8:20. *Then Noah built an altar to the LORD, and took of every clean animal and of every clean bird, and offered burnt offerings on the altar.* The first thing Noah did was to put blood between him and his sins. Thus, Noah walked by the highway of the blood; for this the animals were taken through the flood, and all God's people have been walking that way since, for it is the blood that atones for sin.

Look at Genesis 22:13: *Then Abraham lifted his eyes and looked, and there behind him was a ram caught in a thicket by its horns. So Abraham went and took the ram, and offered it up for a burnt offering instead of his son.* God loved Abraham so much that He spared his son, but He so loved the world that *He did not spare His own Son, but delivered Him up for us all* (Romans 8:32). We are told that Abraham saw Christ's day and was glad (John 8:56). I do not know when he saw it, but I have an idea that it was from this very place that God drew back the curtain of time and showed him Christ as the Bearer of sin. There was the altar, built at the command of Jehovah. God had told him to take his son, his only son whom he loved, and bind and slay him. He had bound the boy. Everything was ready, and he took the knife to kill his son. He did not know what it meant, but *God said it,* and he obeyed. I wish we had men like Abraham now, willing to obey God in the dark, not asking the reason why. I can see him put his arms around his boy as he takes him in his arms and weeps over him. I can hear him telling him the secret he had hidden from him for so long. What a scene! What a struggle it must have been! He was ready to plunge the knife into the heart of his son, but there came a voice from heaven saying, "Abraham! Abraham! Spare your son!" (Genesis 22:11-12). But there was no voice at Calvary, no cry from heaven saying, "Spare your Son." He gave Him up freely for us all, the Innocent for the guilty, the Just for the unjust.

Turn now to Exodus 12 – one of the most important chapters in the Old Testament. We read: *"Now the blood shall be a sign for you on the houses where you are. And when I see the blood, I will pass over you; and the plague shall not be on you to destroy you"* (Exodus 12:13). God did not say, "When I see your good deeds – how you have prayed and wept and groaned – I will pass over you" but *"when I see the blood."* It was not their good resolutions, their tears, their prayers, their works, their faith that saved those men in Egypt; it was the blood. What were they to do to be saved? They were to put the blood on the doorposts and lintel. They were not to put it on the threshold. God did not want them to trample on the blood.

But that is what the world is doing today. Men say it is not the death of Christ; it is His life. But God did not say, "Take a white, spotless lamb and put it there at the front of the door, and when I see the lamb, I will pass over you." Had an Israelite done that, the angel of death would have passed by the lamb, entered that house, and laid his cold hand on the eldest born. A live lamb could not have kept death out that night; he would have fallen a victim like the Egyptian. Very likely, when some of the lords and dukes and great men rode through Goshen and saw the Israelites sprinkling their dwellings, they said they never saw such foolishness. Very likely they thought they were just ruining their houses. Every house had blood on it. No Egyptian could understand it. But on that memorable night when Death entered every house, from the palace of the king to the hovel of the poor, when the wail of sorrow went up from that stricken land, it was the blood that kept him from the homes of Goshen. Yes, it is the blood that must cover our sins. I beg you, do not let the world move you on this point. Let it go on mocking, laughing, and making light of the precious blood of the Son of God. No matter what scoffers may say, this is our only refuge, our only hope.

We cannot cover sin by any good deeds of our own. It is a very common saying, "If I were only as good as that man who has preached the gospel for fifty years or that mother in Israel who has visited the sick and been so kind to the poor, I would feel safe for heaven." But if you are sheltered behind the blood of the Son of God, you are as safe as any saint that ever walked this earth. It is not a long life of good deeds that is going to save us. It is not our Christian usefulness that will ever commend us to God. Certainly, we must work for Christ; it will be better for you in the future if you do. But that is not salvation. You must follow Christ; you must imitate His pure and holy life. I would go further and say it is an *absolute necessity* you should do so; but even though the life of Christ may be preached forever, if His death is left out, it will never save a soul.

People say you must work, work, work to get salvation. Ten thousand times no! You get it as a gift; *whoever desires, let him take* (Revelation 22:17). You can work as much as you like *after* you have taken it. Paul said, *Work out your own salvation* (Philippians 2:12), but he was speaking to Christians, people who had already taken it. So we must first take it, and then we can work it out. We accept salvation as a gift and then begin to work because we cannot help it. All work done before that counts for nothing. When the angel of death swept through the land that night, the good and the bad were destroyed together. The destroying angel came into every house where the blood was not sprinkled. But wherever the blood was on doorpost and lintel, whether they had worked much or whether they had worked none, God passed them over.

The little child in the poorest tent was just as safe as Moses or Aaron, as Joshua or Caleb, as safe as any in the land. God did not say, "When I see your gilded palace or your beautiful home; when I see your goodness, your life of service, or your faith" but *"the blood shall be a sign"* (Exodus 12:13). Not for their own sakes but for Christ's, He passed them by that night. Someone said that the little fly in Noah's ark was just as safe as the great elephant. It was the ark that saved them both. Christ saves the weak disciple just as well as the strong one.

When you go to a train station, you find all classes of people wishing to travel. They have their tickets and take their places in the railcars. When the guard comes to ask for the tickets, he does not look to see what or who you are. You may be rich or poor, educated or uneducated, this or that – but he looks for the tickets, and if you have your ticket, you pass. The ticket is the token or the sign. If you are sheltered behind the blood of Christ, you may be very ignorant or poor in this world, but you are as safe as the wisest or wealthiest.

Many people are wondering why they are so weak, why they fall so often when temptation comes, why so little spiritual power is given to them. I think you will find a lesson in that same chapter: *"Thus you shall eat it: with a belt on your waist, your sandals on your feet, and your staff in your hand. So you shall eat it in haste. It is the LORD's Passover"* (Exodus 12:11). They were not only to kill the lamb and sprinkle the blood on the doorposts, but they were also to *eat* it. That is the

*The reason why we are such sickly Christians is because we do not feed on the Lamb.*

way to get spiritual strength. The reason why we are such sickly Christians is because we do not feed on the Lamb. We have a wilderness journey before us as the children of Israel had, and if we do not feed on Christ, we will starve on the way. We not only have to look to the blood for safety, but we must also feed on Christ for strength.

How much the soul needs to be fed! Day by day our souls must be fed with the heavenly manna. The Lord has given Christ for us; He calls Himself the Bread of Life. Feeding on Christ is feeding on His Word. The Bible is the only book that will feed the soul. If I feed on the Word of God, I get spiritual strength and power. We must live by faith as well as be saved by faith. *"The just shall live by faith"* (Romans 1:17). Daily we must gather the manna. Many people seem to be living on stale manna – manna that they got months or years ago when they were converted. We should no more think of storing up spiritual food to last for ten years than we should of bodily food.

Earlier in the chapter we read, *"This month shall be your*

*beginning of months; it shall be the first month of the year to you*"
(Exodus 12:2). For four hundred years they had been serving
the king of the Egyptians, but God would not let them count
those years. They must make a fresh start. All the years that we
spend in the service of the devil count for nothing. Life never
really begins until we have been sprinkled with the blood of
Christ. Everything dates from the blood, and even Jews must
acknowledge that the death on the cross was the beginning
of days.

Now look at Exodus 29:16: *"And you shall kill the ram, and
you shall take its blood and sprinkle it all around on the altar."*
I used to read these words and the books of the Old Testament,
wondering what they meant. They were to take the blood and
*sprinkle it all around on the altar.* Now I think I understand it.
It teaches that there is no way to approach God without coming
by the blood. It has been so throughout the ages. Even Aaron,
the high priest, had to take blood and sprinkle it around on the
altar before he could meet with God – teaching us the great lesson that approach to God never has been, never will be, never
can be, except through the blood of the Lamb.

We are told this again later in the book: *"And Aaron shall
make atonement upon its horns once a year with the blood of the
sin offering of atonement; once a year he shall make atonement
upon it throughout your generations. It is most holy to the LORD"*
(Exodus 30:10). *Atonement* means "at-one-ment"; the blood
of Christ makes the sinner and God at one. Before Adam fell,
God had bound him to the throne with a golden chain that was
broken by the fall. But Christ came down and linked man back
to God again. *At-one-ment* – that is what the blood of Christ
does; it makes atonement. We talk about sins being forgiven.
They are forgiven, but no sin ever committed in this world
was forgiven without being punished. They were punished in
Christ. He made expiation, atonement: *Who Himself bore our*

*sins in His own body on the tree* (1 Peter 2:24). Think what it cost Christ to make expiation. Think what it cost God when He had to give up His only begotten Son, to give Him up to die!

Look at Leviticus 8:23: *And Moses killed it. Also he took some of its blood and put it on the tip of Aaron's right ear, on the thumb of his right hand, and on the big toe of his right foot.* That is another verse I used to stumble over. What did it mean? Blood on the ear, blood on the hand, blood on the foot? I think I understand it now. *Blood on the ear* – without it, man cannot hear the voice of God. No uncircumcised ear can hear His voice. Men heard the voice of God, and they said it was thunder; they did not know the difference. But when the blood is applied, men know the voice of God – we know that it is the voice of our loving Father in heaven.

*Blood on the hand* – that a man may work for God. Those people who think they are working for God but ignore the blood are deceiving their own souls. One day they will wake up to find that their labor is in vain. Salvation is *to him who does not work but believes on Him* (Romans 4: 5). No one can work his way into the kingdom of God. They said to Christ, *"What shall we do, that we may work the works of God?"* (John 6:28). Perhaps these men had pockets full of money and were ready and willing to build churches. *"This is the work of God,"* said Christ, *"that you believe in Him whom He sent"* (John 6:29). No man or woman can do anything to please God until they have believed in His Son.

Suppose I say to my son, "Willie, I want you to go get me a glass of water." He says he doesn't want to go. "I didn't ask you whether you wanted to go or not, Willie; I told you to go."

"But I don't want to go," he says.

"I say you must go get me a glass of water." He does not want to go. But he knows I am very fond of grapes, and he is very fond of them himself. He goes out, and someone gives him a beautiful cluster of grapes. He comes in and says, "Here, Papa. Here is a beautiful cluster of grapes for you."

"But what about the water?"

"Won't the grapes be acceptable, Papa?"

"No, my boy, the grapes are not acceptable. I won't take them. I want you to get me a glass of water." The little fellow doesn't want to get the water, but he goes out, and this time, someone gives him an orange. He brings it in and places it before me.

"Is that acceptable?" he asks.

"No, no, no!" I say. "I want nothing but water; you cannot do anything to please me until you get the water."

My friends, to please God you must first obey Him; and the first thing He asks us to do is to believe in the Lord Jesus Christ. *Without faith it is impossible to please Him* (Hebrews 11:6). He has given us an unspeakable gift – the Son of His bosom – and if we reject that Son and refuse to follow Him, do you think anything else we can do can please Him?

*Blood on the foot* – to walk with God. God did not walk with the Israelites until the blood was sprinkled in Goshen. Then nothing could stand before them. When they came to the Red Sea, it fled at their approach. In the wilderness, He opened His hand and gave them manna to eat. When they came to the Jordan, they walked with dry feet through the bed of the river because the Almighty God was walking beside them. Yes, it was a blood-bought people that God brought into Canaan, the promised land. And God will walk with every blood-washed sinner, and no man will stand before Him.

I can imagine some of you saying, "I do not understand why God demands blood." A person said to me, "I hate your God; your God demands blood. I don't believe in such a God; *my* God is merciful to all. I do not know your God." But in Leviticus, God tells us why He demands blood: *"For the life of the flesh is in the blood, and I have given it to you upon the altar to make atonement for your souls; for it is the blood that makes atonement for the soul"* (Leviticus 17:11).

Now, suppose Queen Victoria did not want any man to be deprived of his liberty, so she threw all her prisons open and was so merciful that she could not allow anyone to suffer for guilt; how long would she hold the scepter? How long would she rule this empire? Not twenty-four hours. Those very people who cry out about God being merciful would say, "We don't want such a queen." Well, God is merciful, but He is not going to take an unpardoned sinner into heaven.

God demands blood because He said to Adam, *"In the day that you eat of it you shall surely die"* (Genesis 2:17). Then sin came into the world and brought death. God must keep His word. How could God do this and spare the sinner? How could God be just and justify the ungodly? Man has sinned, so man must die. But what if someone would die instead of him? His own life has been forfeited – the wages of sin is death – but what if someone would *buy it back* for him, *He sent His Son to take our nature and die in our place.* would *redeem* him? What if one should come forward and lay down His own life a *ransom for many* – one who had no sins of His own to condemn Him to death (Matthew 20:28)? Glory to God in the highest! *"God so loved the world that He gave His only begotten Son, that whoever believes in Him should not perish but have everlasting life"* (John 3:16). Glory to God in the highest! He sent His Son, born of a woman, to take our nature and die in our place, tasting death for every man (Galatians 4:4). Glory to God in the highest! *The blood of Jesus Christ His Son cleanses us from all sin* (1 John 1:7). If you read your Bibles carefully, you will see the scarlet thread running right through every page. The blood begins to flow in Genesis and runs on to Revelation. That is what God's Book is written for. If you take out the scarlet thread, it would not be worth carrying home.

It is repeated three times in this chapter that the life of the flesh is in the blood. And when God demands blood, in other words, He demands life. It has been forfeited. We have sinned and fallen short of the glory of God. I must die for my sins or find some substitute to die in my place. I cannot get this man or that man to die for me because they have sinned themselves and have to die for their own sins. But Christ was without sin; therefore, He could be my substitute. This is the glorious doctrine of substitution. Christ died for our sins, for mine; and because He died for me, I love Him. Because He died for me, I will serve Him, I will work for Him, I will give Him my very life. He robbed death of its sting and the grave of its victory. The least we can do is give our poor lives to Him.

When the Californian gold fever broke out, a man went there, leaving his wife in New England with their boy. As soon as he was successful, he was to send for them. It was a long time before he succeeded, but at last he got enough money to send for them. The wife's heart leaped for joy. She took her son to New York, got on board a Pacific steamer, and sailed away to San Francisco. They had not been long at sea before the cry of "Fire! Fire!" rang through the ship, and rapidly it gained on them. There was a powder magazine on board, and the captain knew the moment the fire reached the powder, every man, woman, and child would perish. They got out the lifeboats, but they were too small! In a minute they were overcrowded. The last one was just pushing away when the mother pleaded with them to take her and her boy. "No," they said, "we have got as many as we can hold." She entreated them so earnestly that at last they said they would take one more. Do you think she leaped into that boat and left her son to die? No! She seized her boy, gave him one last hug, kissed him, and dropped him over into the boat. "My boy," she said, "if you live to see your father, tell him that I died in your place."

That is a faint type of what Christ has done for us. He laid down His life for us. He died so that we might live. Will you not love Him? What would you say of that young man if he would speak contemptuously of such a mother? She went down to a watery grave to save her son. Will we speak contemptuously of such a Savior? May God make us loyal to Christ! My friends, you will need Him one day. You will need Him when you come to cross the swellings of Jordan. You will need Him when you stand at God's judgment bar. May God forbid that when death draws near, it finds you making light of the precious blood of Christ!

# THE BLOOD - PART 2

## The New Testament

*"Without shedding of blood there is no remission."*
– Hebrews 9:22

We have seen what the Old Testament says about the blood; now let us look at what the New Testament has to say.

In 1 Peter 1:18, we read: *Knowing that you were not redeemed with corruptible things, like silver or gold, from your aimless conduct received by tradition from your fathers, but with the precious blood of Christ, as of a lamb without blemish and without spot.* Silver and gold could not redeem our souls. As I have tried to show, life had been forfeited. Death had come into the world by sin, and nothing but blood could atone for the soul. Therefore, Peter said that we are not redeemed with silver and gold. If gold and silver could have redeemed us, do you not think that God would have created millions of worlds full of gold? It would have been an easy matter for Him. But we are not redeemed by such corruptible things but by the precious blood of Christ. *Redemption* means "buying back." We had sold ourselves for nothing, and Christ redeemed us and bought us back.

A friend in Ireland once met a little Irish boy who had caught a sparrow. The poor little bird was trembling in his hand and seemed very anxious to escape. The gentleman begged the boy to let it go as the bird could not do him any good; but the boy said he would not, for he had chased it three hours before he caught it. He tried to reason it out with the boy but in vain. At last, he offered to buy the bird. The boy agreed to the price, and it was paid. Then the gentleman took the poor little thing and held it out on his hand. The boy had been holding it very tightly, for the boy was stronger than the bird, just as Satan is stronger than we. It sat there for a time, scarcely able to realize the fact that it had liberty; but, in a little while, it flew away chirping, as if to say to the gentleman, "Thank you! Thank you! You have redeemed me." That is what redemption is – buying back and setting free. So Christ came to break the fetters of sin, to open the prison doors, and set the sinner free. This is the good news, the gospel of Christ. You were not redeemed with corruptible things, like silver or gold, but with the precious blood of Christ.

*You are redeemed with the precious blood of Christ.*

"How can I be saved tonight?" you ask. Accept the Redeemer, the Lord Jesus Christ and rest on His finished work. When Christ on Calvary said, *"It is finished,"* it was the shout of the Conqueror. He had come to redeem the world, and now He had done it – done it without money! And His cry to the world comes ringing down the ages today – *"Ho! Everyone who thirsts, come to the waters; and you who have no money, come, buy and eat. Yes, come, buy wine and milk without money and without price"* (Isaiah 55:1).

A few years ago, I was going away to preach one Sunday morning when a young man drove up in front of us. He had an older woman with him.

"Who is that young man?" I asked my friend.

"Do you see that beautiful meadow?" said my friend, "and that land there with the house on it?"

"Yes."

"His father drank that all up," he said. Then he went on to tell me all about him. His father was a great drunk, squandered his property, died, and left his wife in the poorhouse. "And that young man," he said, "is one of the finest young men I ever knew. He has worked hard, earned money, and bought back the land; he has taken his mother out of the poorhouse, and now he is taking her to church."

That is a good illustration. The first Adam, in Eden, sold us for nothing, but the Messiah, the second Adam, came and bought us back again. The first Adam brought us to the poorhouse, as it were; the second Adam makes us kings and priests to God (Revelation 1:6). That is redemption. We get in Christ all that Adam lost and more. Men look on the blood of Christ with scorn and contempt, but the time is coming when the blood of Christ will be worth more than all the kingdoms of the world.

Suppose you were going down to death's gates tonight, going down to the brink of the Jordan without any hope in Christ. If you were a millionaire, what would your millions be worth then? The blood of Christ would be worth more to you than all the silver and gold of the world.

The blood has two cries: it cries either for my condemnation, my damnation; or it cries for my salvation. If I reject the blood of Christ, it cries out for my condemnation. If I accept it, it cries out for pardon and peace. The blood of Abel cried out against his brother Cain (Genesis 4:10). So it was in the days of Christ. When Pilate had Christ on his hands, he said to the Jews, "*What shall I do with Jesus who is called Christ?"* (Matthew 27:22). They cried out, *"Away with Him! Crucify Him!"* (John 19:15). And when he asked which one he should release, Barabbas or Christ, they cried out, *"Barabbas!"* (Matthew 27:17-21). Then when he asked again, "What then shall I do with Him?" a universal shout went up from Jerusalem, "Let Him be crucified! Away with Him! We do not want Him." Pilate turned and washed his hands, and said, *"I am innocent of the blood of this just Person,"* and they cried, *"His blood be on us and on our children"* (Matthew 27:24-25). "We will take the responsibility of it; we will endorse the act. You crucify Him, and let His blood be on us and on our children." Oh, let there be a cry going up, "Let His blood be on us to save, not to condemn."

Look now at Colossians 1:20: *Having made peace through the blood of His cross.* I can tell you there is no peace in the world. There are many rich men, many great men in the world, who do not have peace. I have never seen a man who knew what peace was until he got it at Calvary.

*Having been justified by faith, we have peace with God through our Lord Jesus Christ* (Romans 5:1). Having our sin covered brings peace. There is no peace for the wicked; they are like the troubled sea that cannot rest. Calvary is the place to find peace – peace for the past and grace for the present.

But there is something better still: *And rejoice in hope of the glory of God* (Romans 5:2). Some people think that when they get to Calvary, they have the best; but there is something better in store – glory. I do not know how near it may be to us; it may be that some of us will be ushered very soon into the presence of the King. One gaze at Him will be enough to reward us for all we have had to bear. Yes, there is peace for the past, grace for the present, and glory for the future. These are three things that every child of God ought to have. When the angels came bringing the gospel, they proclaimed, *"Glory to*

*God in the highest, and on earth peace, goodwill toward men!"* (Luke 2:14) That is what the blood brings. It covers and takes away our sin, and it provides peace for the past, grace for the present, and glory for the future.

Now look at John 19:34: *But one of the soldiers pierced His side with a spear, and immediately blood and water came out.* In the book of Zechariah, God foretold that a fountain for sin and uncleanness would be opened for the house of David (Zechariah 13:1). And now we have it opened. The Son of God has been pierced by that Roman soldier's spear. It seems to me that was the crowning act of earth and hell – the crowning act of sin. Look at that Roman soldier as he pushed his spear into the very heart of the God-man. What a hellish deed! But what happened next? Blood covered the spear! Oh! Thank God, the blood covers sin. There was the blood covering that spear – the very point of it. The very crowning act of sin brought out the crowning act of love. The crowning act of wickedness was the crowning act of grace.

A usurper has this world now, but Christ will have it soon. The time of your redemption is drawing near (Luke 21:28). Just a little more suffering, and then He will return to set up His kingdom and reign on the earth. He will rend the heavens (Isaiah 64:1), and His voice will be heard again. He *will descend from heaven with a shout* (1 Thessalonians 4:16). He will sway His scepter from the river to the ends of the earth. The thorn and the brier will be swept away, and the wilderness will rejoice. Let us rejoice; we will see better days. The dreary darkness and sin that sweep along our earth will be done away with. These dark waves of death and hell will be beaten back. Oh, pray that the Lord comes back soon, that the Son of God does not delay.

We will look now at Romans 3:24: *Being justified freely by His grace through the redemption that is in Christ Jesus.* God does what He does freely because He loves to do it. Mark these words: *through the redemption that is in Christ Jesus.* Later we read: *Much more then, having now been justified by His blood, we shall be saved from wrath through Him* (Romans 5:9). The sinner is justified with God by His matchless grace through the blood of His Son. Justified. That means "just as if he had never committed sin." What a wonderful thing – not one sin against him! It is as if he owed someone a debt, and when he went to pay it, he was told, "You owe nothing; it is all settled."

"Why," he would say, "how is that? I got some things from you not long ago, and I want to pay the bill."

"There is nothing against you; you owe nothing."

"But I am sure I got something here."

"There is nothing against you in my ledger; someone else has come and paid it."

That is substitution. Now I know who paid my spiritual debts. It was the Lord Jesus Christ. And God looks at His ledger, and there is nothing against us. Christ was raised for our justification. It is much better to be justified than to be pardoned. Suppose I was arrested for stealing ten thousand dollars. I was tried and found guilty. But suppose the judge had mercy on me and pardoned me. I would come out of prison, but it would be with my head down. I had been found guilty; I could never face the world again. But suppose I was accused of stealing it, but it could not be proved. When the case was tried in court, it was found I had not done anything of the kind. Then I would be *justified*. It would make all the difference in the world. Now God justifies us by the blood of His Son. That is what the blood does – it covers our sin, puts it out of the way, so that nothing is held against us. That is good news.

Revelation 1:5: *To Him who loved us and washed us from our sins in His own blood.* There are many people who wish to be saved but who think they cannot be saved until they get a little better. I met a young man after the service last night who was anxious to be saved, but he thought he could not be because he was not good enough. If you are going to wait until you get rid of your sins, you will never be saved. You cannot get rid of even one sin. Instead of getting better, you will get worse. But thanks be to God, He loves us even in our sins, even before He saves us from our sins. He has loved us and washed us from our sins in His own blood. *Loved us* first, then washed us. But if we attempt to wash ourselves, we will make a miserable mess of it. The blood will cover it all if we only trust ourselves to Christ. *Who shall bring a charge against God's elect?* (Romans 8:33). If He has justified me, it is enough. That is why we like to sing that old hymn:

*The blood will cover it all if we only trust ourselves to Christ.*

> There is a fountain filled with blood
>> Drawn from Immanuel's veins
>>> (William Cowper, "Praise for the Fountain Opened")

Why will it live as long as the church lives on earth? Why will it never die? Why do you hear it sung all over Christendom? I remember how it used to thrill my soul even before I was converted. I could not tell why then yet, but now I know. Thank God, every sin is lost in that fountain. You will find that all these hymns with the scarlet thread in them will live.

Another grand hymn is:

> Rock of Ages, cleft for me,
>> Let me hide myself in Thee;
> Let the water and the blood,
>> From Thy riven side that flowed,
> Be of sin the double cure,
>> Cleanse me from its guilt and power.
>>> (Augustus Toplady, "Rock of Ages")

That hymn speaks of the crucified Christ; it will never get worn out.

Then there is:

> Just as I am, without one plea,
>> But that Thy blood was shed for me,
>> And that Thou bidst me come to Thee,
>>> O Lamb of God, I come.
>>>> (Charlotte Elliott, "Just as I Am")

That is another hymn that will live; you never tire of it. It will be sung on and on, as long as the church is on earth. These hymns are so precious because they tell us about the blood.

Look at Matthew 26:28. It is Christ's own testimony: *"For this is My blood of the new covenant, which is shed for many for the remission of sins."* Paul said, *I declare to you the gospel . . . that Christ died for our sins according to the Scriptures* (1 Corinthians 15:1, 3). Look at Hebrews 9:22: *And without shedding of blood there is no remission.* I would like to ask those who do not believe in the blood, "What are you going to do with your sins?" Would you insult the Almighty by offering Him the fruit of your body to atone for them? Can a man atone for sin? If there is a scoffer here, a man who makes light of the blood, I want to know what he is going to do.

When I was in one of your cities, a gentleman came to me and said, "If you are right, I am wrong; and if I am right, you are wrong."

I saw he was a minister, and I said, "Well, I never heard you preach; if you have heard me, you can tell what the difference is. Where do we differ?"

"Well, you preach that it is the death of Christ; I preach His life. I tell people His death has nothing to do with it; you tell them His life has nothing to do with their salvation and that His death only will save them. I do not believe a word of it."

"Well," I said, "what do you do with this passage: *Who Himself bore our sins in His own body on the tree* (1 Peter 2:24)?"

"Well, I never preached on that text."

"What do you do with this verse: *You were not redeemed with corruptible things, like silver or gold . . . but with the precious blood of Christ* (1 Peter 1:18-19)?"

"I never preached on that text either," was the reply.

"Well, what do you do with this: *Without shedding of blood there is no remission* (Hebrews 9:22)?"

"I never spoke on that," he said.

"What do you do with this: *He was wounded for our transgressions, He was bruised for our iniquities; the chastisement for our peace was upon Him* (Isaiah 53:5)?"

"I never preached on that either."

"What *do* you preach, then?" I asked.

He hesitated for a little and then said, "I preach moral essays."

"You leave out the atonement?"

"Yes."

"Well," I said, "it would all be a sham to me if I did that; I could not understand it. I would go home tomorrow. I would not know what to preach. Moral essays on Christ without His death!"

The young man said, "Well, it does seem a sham sometimes."

He was honest enough to confess that. Why, the whole thing is a myth without the at-one-ment. The crucifixion of Christ is the foundation of the whole matter. If a man is unsound on the blood, he is unsound on everything. *Without shedding of blood there is no remission.*

Look now at Hebrews 10:11. Hebrews is full of the blood. *And every priest stands ministering daily and offering repeatedly the same sacrifices, which can never take away sins. But this Man* [the man Christ Jesus], *after He had offered one sacrifice for sins forever, sat down at the right hand of God.* One sacrifice for sins forever! He has offered Himself as a sacrifice. You no longer need lambs or bulls. The High Priest has offered Himself. The high priest of old could not take his seat; his work was never done. But our great High Priest went up on high and took His seat on the right hand of the Father's throne. The work was done. *"It is finished,"* He said (John 19:30). All those types and shadows are fulfilled in Him, and now they have vanished away.

Look at Mark 14:24: *"This is My blood of the new covenant, which is shed for many."* These are Christ's own words. Connect that with the passage I read from Hebrews: *Without shedding of blood there is no remission.* I believe if a person could get to heaven without the blood of Christ, he would not be happy there. He could not join in the great song that is sung around the throne. He could not sing the song of Moses and the Lamb. He could not say he was redeemed by the blood of the Lamb. He would be away in some corner, out of tune with the rest. He would not be in harmony with them, and he would not wish to stay there. But a person cannot get there without the blood; the only way is by the new and living way that Christ has opened.

Look again for a minute at Hebrews 10:19: *Therefore, brethren, having boldness to enter the Holiest by the blood of Jesus, by a new and living way which He consecrated for us, through the veil, that is, His flesh.* Before Christ died, the Jews had to have the high priest intercede for them. He used to go once a year into the holy of holies with blood to make intercession, but since Christ, our great High Priest, came, we do not need any Aaron to intercede for us. When Christ died, He opened a new and living way. He made us all kings and priests. It is said that the veil that was torn was His flesh. When He cried on the cross, *"It is finished,"* the veil of the temple was torn in two. God seized it with His right hand and tore it away. There is no longer a veil between God and man! We need no bishop, no pope, no priest to intercede for us now. Christ has died and is risen again. We are all kings and priests now; we can go straight to the holy of holies ourselves. We need no man to intercede for our souls. The moment a person is saved by the blood, he becomes a king and a priest. God calls him "My son." He is an heir to heaven and of glory. He is redeemed by the blood; he is brought near by the blood. By the blood, he gains victory over the world, the flesh, and the devil.

There is a very somber passage in Hebrews 10: *Anyone who has rejected Moses' law dies without mercy on the testimony of two or three witnesses. Of how much worse punishment, do you suppose, will he be thought worthy who has trampled the Son of God underfoot, counted the blood of the covenant by which he was sanctified a common thing, and insulted the Spirit of grace?* (Hebrews 10:28-29). If a man despised Moses's law, they led him out and stoned him to death. Sinner, let me ask you, what are you going to do with the blood of God's only Son? It is a terrible thing to make light of the blood, to laugh and ridicule the doctrine of the blood. I would rather *It is a terrible thing to make light of the blood.* fall dead on this platform than do such a thing. It makes my heart shudder when I hear men speak lightly of it.

Some time ago, a thought made a deep impression on my mind. The only thing that Christ left of His body on the earth was His blood. He took His flesh and bones away. But when He went up on high, He left His blood down here. What are you going to do with the blood? Are you going to make light of this blood, to trample on it? May God give us all a glimpse of Christ crucified tonight!

I wish I had time to go on and talk about the blood in Revelation; it is full of it. *"They overcame him by the blood of the Lamb and by the word of their testimony"* (Revelation 12:11). The only way to overcome the devil, the lion of hell, is by the blood of the Lamb. The devil knows that the moment a poor sinner flees to the blood, he is beyond his reach.

As I have traveled up and down Christendom, I have found that a minister who gives clear teaching on this doctrine is successful. A man who covers up the cross, though he may be an intellectual man and draw large crowds, will have no life there, and his church will be only a gilded sepulcher. But God honors those men who preach the doctrine of the cross, who make much of the blood, and hold up Christ as the sinner's only hope of heaven and only substitute; souls are always saved in the church where the blood of Christ is preached. May God help us to make much of the blood of His Son.

It cost God so much to give us His Son: should we try to keep Him from the world that is perishing because they do not know Him? The world can get along without us but not without Christ. Let us preach Christ in season and out of season (2 Timothy 4:2). Let us go to the sick and dying and hold up the Savior who came to seek and save them, who died to redeem them. *"They overcame him by the blood of the Lamb and by the word of their testimony."*

Let us look at one last verse: *"These are the ones who come out of the great tribulation, and washed their robes and made them white in the blood of the Lamb"* (Revelation 7:14). Sinner, how are you going to get your robes clean if you do not get them washed in the blood of the Lamb? How are you going to wash them? Can you make them clean? I pray that we may all get back to the paradise above. There they sing the sweet song of redemption. May each of us join them. At most, it will be only a few years before we will be there to sing the sweet song of Moses and the Lamb. But if you die without Christ, without hope, and without God, where will you be? O sinner, be wise; do not make light of the blood.

On his death bed, an elderly minister of the gospel said, "Bring me the Bible." Putting his finger on the verse *The blood of Jesus Christ His Son cleanses us from all sin,* he said, "I die in the hope of this verse" (1 John 1:7). It was not his fifty years' preaching, but the blood of Christ. May God grant that when we come at last to stand before the great white throne, our robes may be washed in the cleansing blood of Christ!

# HEAVEN - PART I

*I heard a loud voice from heaven saying, "Behold, the tabernacle of God is with men, and He will dwell with them, and they shall be His people. God Himself will be with them and be their God."*
– Revelation 21:3

Some time ago, on my way to a meeting, a friend asked what I was going to speak about. I told him I thought I would preach about heaven. He seemed very disappointed and replied that he hoped I would talk about something practical; there would be time enough to talk about heaven when we got there.

I think if God did not want us to know anything about heaven, He would not have written so much about it. And if heaven is to be our future home, we should try to learn all we can about it so that we may live more for it. If we were about to emigrate to a distant land, we would never tire of hearing about it. We would wish to know all about its people, its climate and resources, its schools and institutions, its advantages for children, and its prospects for business. We would be interested in everything. When we are going to spend eternity in another world, can we know or hear too much about it?

Christians are often asked why they address their prayers *upward,* as if God's dwelling place were any more above than around them. But I think it is right to locate heaven and to locate it above. In Deuteronomy we read: *"Look down from Your holy habitation, from heaven, and bless Your people Israel"* (Deuteronomy 26:15). *Look down* from heaven. Then in Genesis we are told that God *went up* from talking with Abraham – *went up* (Genesis 17:22). And Christ Himself, the only One who can really tell us about heaven because He has been there, what does He say? John records His words to Nicodemus: *"No man has ascended to heaven but He who came down from heaven, that is, the Son of Man who is in heaven"* (John 3:13). Again, we are told in the book of Mark: *Looking up to heaven, He sighed* (Mark 7:34). And when His work was over here and He was returning to the many mansions of His Father's house, standing in the midst of the loved ones for whom He was going to prepare a place, *He was taken up, and a cloud received Him out of their sight* (Acts 1:9).

Heaven is the dwelling place of God. This, after all, is the great point. It matters little how far away it is. God is there, and that is enough. We are sure it is not so far away that He cannot hear the humblest sigh of prayer or watch the gathering tears of repentance trembling on the sinner's cheek. And man, too, can look from earth to heaven. When God opens his eyes and draws aside the veil, like He did for Stephen, he can see right into it: *He, being full of the Holy Spirit, gazed into heaven and saw the glory of God, and Jesus standing on the right hand of God, and said, "Look! I see the heavens opened and the Son of Man standing at the right hand of God!"* (Acts 7:55-56). Stephen discovered the secret of the attractiveness of heaven. He saw Christ at the right hand of God. The King in His beauty was there, and that makes heaven heaven.

Someone was asked what he expected to do when he got to heaven. He replied that he thought he would take one good look at Christ for about five hundred years, and then he might look around for the apostles, saints, and martyrs. It seems to me that one glimpse of Him who loved us and washed us in His blood will repay us for all we suffer here in this dark world.

A little child whose mother was dying was taken away to live with some friends because it was thought she did not understand what death is. All the while, the child wanted to go home to see her mother. At last, when the funeral was over and she was taken home, she ran all over the house, searching the sitting room, the parlor, the library, and the bedrooms. She went from one end of the house to the other, and when she could not find her mother, she wished to be taken back to where they brought her

*Heaven would be no heaven if Christ were not there.*

from. Home had lost its attraction for the child when her mother was not there. My friends, the great attraction in heaven will not be its pearly gates, its golden streets, nor its choir of angels, but it will be Christ. Heaven would be no heaven if Christ were not there. But we know that He is at the right hand of the Father, and our eyes will gaze on Him soon; we will be satisfied when we awake with His likeness.

But Jesus is not there alone – our friends are there. God the Father is there, Christ the Son is there, angels are there, and in Revelation 7, we read of *a great multitude which no one could number, of all nations, tribes, peoples, and tongues.* We read of the redeemed who stand *before the throne and before the Lamb, clothed with white robes, with palm branches in their hands* (Revelation 7:9). Yes, we have friends in heaven.

A bereaved father asked me the other day if I thought the little one he had lost had gone to be with Jesus. I could only tell him what David said when he lost his son: *"I shall go to him, but he shall not return to me"* (2 Samuel 12:23). It is a very sweet thought to me, and it must be to you also who have lost little ones, that the King can take better care of them than we can. If we could look into the eternal city, we would see the Shepherd leading them by the green pastures and the still waters. He will care for each little lost lamb far better than its own fond mother; and is it not sweeter for them to be forever with the Lord than down in this sad land of suffering and sin? Our friends are not lost, just gone ahead. They have had the *desire to depart and be with Christ, which is far better* (Philippians 1:23), and He has gratified it. Although to live was to live for Christ, yet to be with Him was, even to Paul, *far better.*

But there is still more in heaven. One time the disciples had been out preaching and had wonderful success. They had great power, had cast out devils, and worked many miracles. They came back elated. Like workers in a great revival, they were filled with joy and celebration. But Christ said, *"Do not rejoice in this, that the spirits are subject to you, but rather rejoice because your names are written in heaven"* (Luke 10:20). What a glorious thought! Our names are written in heaven. We can be sure of it. If the children of God cannot *know* that their names are written in heaven, how are they to rejoice? If there had been any doubt about it, how could the disciples have rejoiced when Christ told them to rejoice? If we are Christians, it is our privilege not only to know it, to be quite sure of it, but also to rejoice in it.

*Is my name written in heaven?* is life's grand question. Is my name in the Book of Life? Not if your name is in the church records; that record may not be kept in the same way that the record in heaven is kept. And there may be names in the church record that have never been written in heaven. But it is God's record we are talking about. God keeps a record, a book of the lost and a book of the saved, a book of the living and a book of the dead. Which book is your name in? Can you rejoice at this moment that your name is written in the Book of Life? This question is important: *Anyone not found written in the Book of Life was cast into the lake of fire* (Revelation 20:15). But of heaven it is said, *There shall by no means enter it anything that defiles, or causes an abomination or a lie, but only those who are written in the Lamb's Book of Life* (Revelation 21:27).

Recently, some traveling friends arrived at an English hotel but found that it had been full for days. They were getting ready to leave to look for another place to stay, when one of the ladies told the others goodbye and said she intended to remain there.

"How can that be," they asked, "when you heard that the hotel is full?"

"Oh," she replied, "I called ahead a number of days ago, and my room has been secured."

My friend, send your name on ahead, and the door of heaven can never be shut against you. It is a wise precaution. Then everything will be ready for you. When the journey of life is over, you will mount up as with angel wings and inherit the kingdom prepared from the foundation of the world. Many are spending their time and strength on a home down here, with its shallow luxuries and fleeting joys. But what will all the mansions of earth do for you if you have not secured a title to a mansion in the sky?

A soldier, wounded during our last war, lay dying on his cot. Suddenly, the deathlike stillness of the room was broken by the cry, "Here! Here!" that burst from the lips of the dying man. Friends rushed to the spot and asked what he wanted. "Listen," he said. "They are calling the roll of heaven, and I am answering to my name." A few moments later, he whispered, "Here!" and passed into the presence of the King.

If we have made sure that our own names are written in heaven, the next most important thing is to be sure that our children's names are there. The promise is not to you only but to your children. Mother, is the name of that boy of yours written in the Lamb's Book of Life? It is better that your children's names are written there than that you secure for them great possessions on this dark earth. Oh, I pity the son who has never had an interest beyond the grave but *May God make fathers* more the mother who has never told *and mothers more faithful* him of the rest that endures for the *and truer to their duty.* people of God. May God make fathers and mothers more faithful and truer to their duty to see that their children grow up to be a blessing to the world and that their family circle is unbroken when they meet in heaven!

Whenever I think about this subject, two fathers come to mind. One lived on the Mississippi River. He was a man of great wealth, yet he would have freely given it all to bring back his eldest boy from his early grave. One day that boy had been carried home unconscious. They did everything they could to restore him but in vain.

"He will die," said the doctor.

"But, doctor," said the agonized father, "can you do nothing to bring him to consciousness, even for a moment?"

"Perhaps," said the doctor; "but he will not live."

Time passed, and after waiting in suspense, the father's wish was gratified. "My son," he whispered, "the doctor tells me you are dying."

"Well," said the boy, "you never prayed for me, Father. Won't you pray for my lost soul now?"

The father wept. It was true he had never prayed. He was a stranger to God. And in a little while, that unprayed for soul passed into its dark eternity. O Father! If *your* boy were dying and called on you to pray, could you lift your burdened heart to heaven? Have you learned this sweetest lesson of heaven or earth, to know and hold communion with your God? And before this evil world has marked your dearest treasures as its prey, have you learned to lead your little ones to Christ?

What a contrast is the other father! He, too, had a lovely boy, and one day he came home to find him at the gates of death.

"A great change has come over our boy," said the weeping mother; "he was only a little ill before, but it seems now he is dying fast." The father went into the room and placed his hand on the forehead of the little boy. He could see the boy *was* dying. He could feel the cold damp of death.

"My son, do you know you are dying?"

"No; am I?"

"Yes; you are dying."

"Will I die today?"

"Yes, my boy, you cannot live until night."

"Well, then, I will be with Jesus tonight, won't I, Dad?"

"Yes, my son, you will spend tonight with the Savior." As he turned away, the little fellow saw the tears trickling over his father's cheeks.

"Don't weep for me, Dad," he said. "When I get to heaven, I will go straight to Jesus and tell Him that ever since I can remember you have tried to lead me to Him."

God has given me one little boy, and if God would take him, I would rather have him carry a testimony like that to my Master than have all the wealth of the world placed at his feet.

Mothers and Fathers, the little ones can understand early; be earnest with them now. You do not know how soon you may be taken from them or they may be taken from you, so impress on their minds that you care for their souls a million times more than for their worldly prospects. And if you yourself have never thought how little it would profit you to gain the whole world and lose your own soul, I beg you not to let another sun go down before you are able to say that *your* name has been written in heaven.

# HEAVEN - PART 2

*"Do not lay up for yourselves treasures on earth, where moth and rust destroy and where thieves break in and steal; but lay up for yourselves treasures in heaven."*
– Matthew 6:19-20

We have seen that God is in heaven, for it is His dwelling place and that Christ is there, for He is at the right hand of the Father. We have seen that the redeemed saints are there and that our names are there. If we are true Christians, we ought to have our *treasure* there also. We are commanded to put our treasure in heaven: *"Do not lay up for yourselves treasures on earth, where moth and rust destroy and where thieves break in and steal; but lay up for yourselves treasures in heaven, where neither moth nor rust destroys and where thieves do not break in and steal"* (Matthew 6:19-20).

If our treasure were in heaven, we would not have to be urging men to live for heaven or pleading with them to lift their hearts toward heaven. Their hearts would be there already. *"Where your treasure is, there your heart will be also"* (Matthew 6:21).

It does not take long to find out where a man's treasure is; you have only to watch where his heart is. The man who makes politics his god, see how his face lights up the moment you talk about it! If you put a man whose heart is set on business in the way of making a few thousands even at the risk of losing a few more, he thinks you have done him the greatest favor in the world. The eyes of the man whose god is pleasure sparkle when you even mention it. One would think from such men that there is nothing worth living for but politics, business, and pleasure. But talk to a child of God whose treasures are in heaven, and you will find that the world hardly interests him. He will tell you that he has here no continuing city (Hebrews 13:14), that he is a stranger and a pilgrim (Hebrews 11:13), and that heaven is his home. And as he talks of Christ, the promises, and the hope beyond the grave, you see that he enjoys the heavenly calm that the world does not know.

When I was on the Pacific Coast, I spent my first Sunday in San Francisco. I went to Sunday school, but it was a very wet, stormy day. So few teachers and students showed up that the superintendent wondered whether he should send everyone home. However, as they had come through the rain, it was decided that we would go on with the lesson, and I was asked to lead. The subject happened to be "Our Treasures in Heaven." The blackboard was readied, and being a poor writer myself, I handed the chalk to one of the teachers and said to the children, "Now, I want you to tell me some earthly treasures; what do you suppose men think most of?"

Someone cried, "Money."

"Put that down," I said. "Anything else?"

"Land."

"Put that down."

Many strange things were said: one little boy said, "Rum," and perhaps he was nearer the truth than any of them, for many men will sell soul and body, business and family, and home and everything else for drink. When that list was finished, I asked them next to give me a list of heavenly treasures. The first answer was "Jesus," and as we went on from one to another, we found that the treasures of heaven were far more numerous and much more precious than all the treasures that the earth could give.

The young man who was writing down the answers was an unconverted teacher. As he scanned the lists and compared the earthly with the heavenly, he stood transfixed with shame. "What a fool have I been!" he said to himself. "I have come to the Pacific Coast and spent what I had for such things of earth!" And there at that blackboard, he vowed to God that for the rest of his life, his heart would be set alone on the things that are above.

*We bring nothing into this world, and it is certain we will carry nothing out.*

Think with me for a moment about what earthly treasures are. Suppose we set our hearts on money. When misfortune darts across our path, we fight to hold on to our money, but the brief struggle, which the world knows so well, is soon over, and then we are beggars! Try reputation. In one evil moment, we may lose the little we have gained; or those who have never had any of their own may steal ours away with the tongue of slander. If we are looking to our children for our principal joy, we cannot count on that lasting; for death may carry them away, or worse than death, disgrace may count them with the living dead. And even if we were to have all the money we could want, the best reputation, and the most lovely and loved children – is it not true that we have provided for only a few brief years while all of eternity has been uncared for or forgotten?

*"Do not lay up for yourselves treasures on earth."* It looks a little stern, perhaps, but it must be right. After all, all that a man is really worth is what he has in heaven. We bring nothing

into this world, and it is certain we will carry nothing out. So God says to not lay up treasures here. The Christian who does, suffers. There is no reward in it. It is done at a terrible expense. We trade the heart's desire for the soul's leanness.

Two ships are coming up a river. The first, full sail, cuts bravely through the water. The second creeps along towed by another. She appears to be on the point of sinking, but still she floats. Why? Because she has a cargo of timber and has become waterlogged. Lot was all right while he stayed with his Uncle Abraham, but when he left him and went down into Sodom, he got many of this world's goods and grew waterlogged. So it is with many Christians. They are waterlogged. They have so much money that they cannot get into the harbor themselves, and they require others to help them in. The religious life gets sluggish. The spiritual pulse begins to beat slowly. "Why is it?" they say, "that I do not have more spiritual power and more joy in the Lord?" The secret is easily discovered. People who ask these questions have their treasure here.

When men go up in balloons, they take with them bags of sand for ballast; and when they want to rise higher, they throw out some of the sand. There are some Christians who, before they rise higher, will have to throw out some ballast. It may be money or some other worldly consideration, but if they wish to rise, they must get rid of it. If you are overloaded, just throw out a little money, and you will mount up as on eagle's wings. Any minister will tell you what to do with it. I never saw any department of the Lord's work that did not need money.

A friend of mine called on a wealthy Illinois farmer to get him interested in a soldiers' mission. The farmer took him up on the cupola of his house and said, "Look over that beautiful rolling prairie; that is all mine, as far as the eye can see." He took him to another view and, pointing over the rich farms of the Mississippi Valley, showed him pastureland for thirty miles around, with large herds of cattle, horses, and sheep. "They are all mine," he said. "I have made it all myself." Then he pointed proudly toward the town and showed him streets and buildings and a great hall named after himself, and he said once more, "They are all mine. I came here a poor man, but my own hard work has done it all."

My friend said nothing; but when he had seen it all, he raised his finger and pointed solemnly to the sky. "What," he said, "do you have up there?"

The rich man's face fell. "Where?" he asked.

"In heaven."

"I do not have anything there." He had lived his threescore years and ten and would soon enter eternity, but he had no treasure there.

"Is it not strange," said my friend, "a man of your judgment and forethought, making such a wreck of life, living for the moment and on borrowed time, to die a beggar and enter eternity a pauper!" But a few months after that, he died as he had lived, and his property went to others.

O my friends, if there are any of you living for this world alone, remember that death will part you and your treasures forever. I beg you to ask yourself what provision you have made for the other life. Is your heart set on your little boy? Is he your god, the idol of your life? Or is it your money, your name, your things, or position in society? Then you are disobeying the law of Him who will one day be your Judge. *"Do not lay up for yourselves treasures on earth."*

There is another thought I would like you to look at. Our *rest* is to be in heaven. Hebrews 4:9 says, *There remains therefore a rest for the people of God.* That is another treasure we are to have in heaven. Let us not talk of rest down here; we have all eternity to rest in. What we want is to be faithful in the few months or years that we are here, and then we will rest as eternal ages roll on. This is the place for *work*. *"Blessed are the dead who die in the Lord . . . that they may rest from their labors, and their works follow them"* (Revelation 14:13). Our works will follow us.

If we are faithful, we will leave a record behind us before the night comes. We can set streams running here in this dark world that will flow on after we have gone to heaven.

Twenty-five hundred years have passed since Daniel lived, but he lives today. His light shines out brightly all over Christendom! We love to read about his life. It inspires and cheers us as we read of him standing up for God in Babylon. His works follow him.

Many people have made a sad mistake. They think the church is a sort of resting place. They join a church, and that is about the last we hear of them. They think that a good Christian has nothing more to do than get a good pew in a respectable place of worship, and all the work after that is to hear a sermon a week.

But, my friends, do not think of rest and pleasure down here. We will rest when Christ comes but not until then. The time will come when the wicked will cease from troubling, and the weary will be at rest (Job 3:17).

I heard of a Christian who did not succeed in his work as well as he used to, and he wished to die and go home. One night he dreamed that he had died and was carried by the angels to the eternal city. As he went along the crystal pavement of heaven, he met a man he used to know, and they went walking down the golden streets together. All at once he noticed everyone looking in the same direction and saw One coming up who was fairer than the sons of men. It was his blessed Redeemer. As the chariot came opposite to them, Jesus came over. Calling to the one friend, He placed him in His own chariot seat, but the first man He led aside. Pointing over the walls of heaven, He told the man to look and asked him what he saw.

"It seems to be the dark earth I have come from."

"What else?"

"I see men, as if they were blindfolded, going over a terrible precipice into a bottomless pit.

"Well," said He, "will you remain up here and enjoy those mansions that I have prepared or go back to that dark earth and warn these men and tell them about Me and My kingdom and the rest that remains for the people of God?"

That man never wished himself dead again. He wanted to live as long as he could to tell men of heaven and of Christ. That is what God wants us to do. We will rest soon; we have all eternity to rest in. But the church is the place for work, and as soon as our work is done, there will be the voice calling us, "Come up here."

And then – for there is still something else in heaven – we will get our *crown*. *There is laid up for me the crown of righteousness, which the Lord, the righteous Judge, will give to me on that Day* (2 Timothy 4:8). There is a crown laid up for every one of His children. God has promised it. *"Be faithful until death, and I will give you the crown of life"* (Revelation 2:10). What did Paul run for? Salvation? Ten thousand times no; he got that at the cross. That was settled long ago. Paul ran for a *crown*. There will be many who will get into heaven, but they will have no crown – crownless Christians. I never read the story of Paul or even hear his name mentioned without feeling ashamed of myself. If I may be allowed the expression, Satan met his match when he met Paul. He was never able to get him off the right track. Paul kept his eye right on Christ, and now he wears His crown.

"Paul, why are you so ambitious – to make a name for yourself? Why are you so desperately serious?"

"I am running for my crown," says Paul.

"Do you hear what they say about you, that you are a mere babbler attempting to turn the world upside down (Acts 17:18)? They have made up their minds to kill you. The Jews say all kinds of things against you."

"I know it," says Paul, "but none of these things move me."
Stand by his side again. He has received thirty-nine stripes;
he has been beaten four times, and now he is to be beaten again.

"If you get out of this difficulty, what will you do, Paul?"

"Do?" says Paul. "I do only one thing – *I press toward the
goal for the prize of the upward call of God in Christ Jesus*"
(Philippians 3:14). What did he care about being beaten? "You
don't think," he says, "that these afflictions are going to stop me?"

Why, if we received one stripe on our backs, how we would
whine! I do not know how many volumes of books would be
written about it. We would be called martyrs, yet Paul calls
them *light afflictions* (2 Corinthians 4:17).

Stand next to Paul again. This time, they have stoned him.
He is bruised and bleeding, but the great warrior rises up and
puts on his armor again. What is he going to do?

"You survived this, Paul. What are you going to do next?"

"Do?" he cries once more. "I do just *one* thing – *I press toward
the goal for the prize*. I do not want to lose my crown." He never
turns to the right hand or to the left. He fixes his eye right on
the crown. "There is laid up for me a crown that cannot fade."

Look at him again. He goes to Macedonia, and the first thing
he gets in Philippi is the jail. If that happened to any Christian
now, what an outcry there would be! What moaning and wail-
ing there would be inside the prison! What scheming to get
out, what claims for damages! But that is not the way this old
warrior looks at it.

"Silas!" he says at midnight; "it is time to have our evening
worship." And there in that prison cell, with bleeding backs
and feet tight in the stocks, they sing their psalm of praise.
It would be about the last place we would think of singing
praises, and if we did sing, it would be some melancholy hymn!
But not Paul. "If God wants me to go to heaven by way of the
Philippian prison," he says, "it is all the same to me. Rejoice

and be glad, Silas. I thank God that I am counted worthy to suffer for Jesus's sake."

And as they sang their praises to God, the other prisoners heard them. What was far more important, the Lord heard them; the prison shook, their chains fell off, and they were free men (Acts 16)! We talk about Alexander the Great making the world tremble with his armies, but here is a little tentmaker who made the world tremble without an army!

Then look at the end of Paul's glorious life. He was in Rome and about to be executed. He picked up his pen and wrote to Timothy: *The time of my departure is at hand. I have fought the good fight, I have finished the race, I have kept the faith* (2 Timothy 4:6-7). Thank God he kept the faith! He did not break away and teach false doctrine. He believed in the gospel that Christ died and that men must believe on the Lord Jesus Christ if they want to be saved. *There is laid up for me the crown.* I would have liked to have been in Rome when Paul was there; there was something there worth seeing then. I would have liked to see him walking down those streets. Rome never saw such a conqueror as that man.

"Paul! You are going to your execution; are you not sorry that you gave your life to the Lord Jesus? You have had to suffer so much. You were stoned, persecuted, beaten with many stripes, in many dangers in the wilderness, in perils by sea and land – are you not sorry? Would you give your life to Christ if you had it to live over again?"

"Yes," he replies, "if I had ten thousand lives, I would willingly give them all for His dear sake." He has nothing to regret, nothing to be sorry for. "Sorry?" he cries. "I thank God a thousand times a day that I gave myself to Him!"

Look at him as he marches along to execution like a conqueror. If you had taken your stand by his side, you might have heard him whisper, "I will be absent from the body and present with the Lord tonight" (2 Corinthians 5:8). He has no worldly wealth to trouble him – perhaps a few tools that he used in tentmaking – but in heaven, he has treasures untold, and he prepares to go for his crown. You can see a smile on his face as he lays his head on the guillotine, and his soul leaps into the chariot of fire that stands by its side.

*I do not believe a man will be used much by God until he is above the thought of receiving rewards from men.*

I can imagine them watching for him from the tops of the walls of heaven, and there is a "Hallelujah!" as he sweeps away up to the throne. And I can hear the shout of the Master as he enters the pearly gates, "Well done, Paul. You have fought a good fight, you have kept the faith, you have finished the work that was given you to do; enter into the joy of your Lord!" (Matthew 25:23). The Master rises and places the crown on his brow, but he takes it and casts it at the feet of his Lord.

Paul got his reward at last. Down here it was tribulation, but I have an idea that he thanks God more today for his afflictions than for his prosperity. John Bunyan thanked God more for Bedford Jail than for anything that ever happened to him. And Paul, in prison, took out his pen and wrote these letters which have come down as a blessing through the ages. The streams of grace that Paul set running are running still. Eighteen hundred years have passed since He wrote these letters to the churches, but their fruits are still going up from every region and nation. So if things go against us, let us thank God. Our reward is ahead. I do not believe a man will be used much by God until he is above the thought of receiving rewards from men. *"Rejoice and be exceedingly glad, for great is your reward in heaven"* (Matthew 5:12). If God calls it *great*, it must be something worth having. Do not spoil it by seeking the world's honors.

Not long ago there lived an old bedridden saint. A Christian lady who visited her found her always very cheerful. This visitor had a lady friend of wealth who constantly looked on the dark side of things and was always sad and depressed even though she was a professed Christian. She thought it would do this lady good to see the bedridden saint, so she took her down to the house. She lived up in the garret, five stories up, and when they had got to the first story, the lady picked up the hem of her dress and said, "How dark and filthy it is!"

"It's better higher up," said her friend. They got to the next story, and it was no better; the lady complained again, but her friend replied, "It's better higher up." At the third floor, it seemed still worse, and the lady kept complaining, but her friend kept saying, "It's better higher up." At last they got to the fifth story, and when they went into the sickroom, there was a nice carpet on the floor, flowering plants in the window, and little birds singing. And there they found this bedridden saint – one of those saints whom God is polishing for His own temple – just beaming with joy. The lady said to her "It must be very hard for you to lie here." She smiled and said, "It's better higher up." Yes! If things go against us, my friends, let us remember that it's better higher up.

I was going to New Orleans from Chicago a few years ago, and there were two ladies in the train car with me. They were well acquainted with one another by the time they reached Cairo, where one lived. The other was going on to New Orleans. The one who had to get out at Cairo said to the other, "I wish you would stay here with me for a few days. I like your company so much."

"I would like to stay," replied the other, "but my things are all packed up and have gone on ahead of me; I have no clothes but those I am wearing. They are *good enough to travel in*, but I would not like to be seen in company with them."

It is the same with the Christian. He is away from home here, his treasure has gone on ahead, and anything is *good enough to travel in.* If things don't go smoothly down here, we do not need to be too particular, they're *good enough to travel in.* If our treasures are in heaven, our hearts will be there, and we will be living as pilgrims and strangers on the earth.

One more thought. What causes joy in heaven? If Queen Victoria left her throne today, what intense excitement there would be! Queen Victoria leaving the throne! It would stir the nations of the earth. The whole world would know about it. But I do not know that it would be noticed in heaven. But if there were one little boy down here converted today, heaven would notice. Jesus Christ said there is joy in heaven over *one* sinner who repents (Matthew 15:7).

My little boy, don't you want to become a lamb for the Shepherd to watch over and care for? My little girl, don't you want to become a daughter of heaven, a follower of Christ?

It may be that at this moment every wall of heaven is alive with the redeemed. There is a mother watching for her daughter. Daughter! Can you not see her? She is calling you now to the better land. Have you no response to that long-hushed voice that has prayed for you so often? Young man, are there no voices there that prayed for *you?* Are there none whom you promised to meet again, if not on earth, in heaven? Which of you, fathers and mothers, can hear in the angels' chorus the music of the little ones you loved, who have winged their way to be in glory forever with the Lord? Oh, turn your backs on the world, fall on your knees, and ask God for Christ's sake to write *your* name in the Lamb's Book of Life so that we and those we love may live forever with the Lord!

# DWIGHT L. MOODY
# – A BRIEF BIOGRAPHY

D wight Lyman Moody was born on February 5, 1837, in Northfield, Massachusetts. His father died when Dwight was only four years old, leaving his mother with nine children to care for. When Dwight was seventeen years old, he left for Boston to work as a salesman. A year later, he was led to Jesus Christ by Edward Kimball, Moody's Sunday school teacher. Moody soon left for Chicago and began teaching a Sunday school class of his own. By the time he was twenty-three, he had become a successful shoe salesman, earing $5,000 in only eight months, which was a lot of money for the middle of the nineteenth century. Having decided to follow Jesus, though, he left his career to engage in Christian work for only $300 a year.

D. L. Moody was not an ordained minister, but was an effective evangelist. He was once told by Henry Varley, a British evangelist, "Moody, the world has yet to see what God will do with a man fully consecrated to Him."

Moody later said, "By God's help, I aim to be that man."

It is estimated that during his lifetime, without the help of television or radio, Moody traveled more than one million miles, preached to more than one million people, and personally dealt with over seven hundred and fifty thousand individuals.

D. L. Moody died on December 22, 1899.

Moody once said, "Some day you will read in the papers that D. L. Moody, of East Northfield, is dead. Don't you believe a word of it! At that moment I shall be more alive than I am now. I shall have gone up higher, that is all – out of this old clay tenement into a house that is immortal; a body that death cannot touch, that sin cannot taint, a body fashioned like unto His glorious body. I was born of the flesh in 1837. I was born of the Spirit in 1856. That which is born of the flesh may die. That which is born of the Spirit will live forever."

# OTHER SIMILAR TITLES

*The Way to God*
by Dwight L. Moody

There is life in Christ. Rich, joyous, wonderful life. It is true that the Lord disciplines those whom He loves and that we are often tempted by the world and our enemy, the devil. But if we know how to go beyond that temptation to cling to the cross of Jesus Christ and keep our eyes on our Lord, our reward both here on earth and in heaven will be 100 times better than what this world has to offer.

This book is thorough. It brings to life the love of God, examines the state of the unsaved individual's soul, and analyzes what took place on the cross for our sins. *The Way to God* takes an honest look at our need to repent and follow Jesus, and gives hope for unending, joyous eternity in heaven.

*Available where books are sold.*

### The Overcoming Life
### by Dwight L. Moody

**Overcome your greatest enemy, yourself.**

Are you an overcomer? Or, are you plagued by little sins that easily beset you? Even worse, are you failing in your Christian walk, but refuse to admit and address it? No Christian can afford to dismiss the call to be an overcomer. The earthly cost is minor; the eternal reward is beyond measure.

Dwight L. Moody is a master at unearthing what ails us. He uses stories and humor to bring to light the essential principles of successful Christian living. Each aspect of overcoming is looked at from a practical and understandable angle. The solution Moody presents for our problems is not religion, rules, or other outward corrections. Instead, he takes us to the heart of the matter and prescribes biblical, God-given remedies for every Christian's life. Get ready to embrace genuine victory for today, and joy for eternity.

*Available where books are sold.*